AF491645

ISBN: 979-8-9899283-2-3 Paperback
ISBN: 979-8-9899283-3-0 EBook

Cover and Interior Design by Stewart A. Williams
Copyedit by Brooks Becker

Printed in the United States of America
First Printing edition 2025
The PineLands Company, Publisher
New Wilmington, Pennsylvania

Author's Note

The five stories in *The Farm* include two that are autobiographical—"Growing Up with Lady of Spain" and "The Christmas Kid"—and three that are pure fiction.

Exactly what inspired me to put these stories together, I cannot say for certain. As you read through this relatively short work, you may discover a thread that knits them together. Some might say these are "coming of age" or "rite of passage" pieces, or just odd bits of mystery or inspiration. Or some might suggest these stories might apply to an entire life's passage. For Strand fans out there, my favorite detectives make a cameo appearance in the first story, which takes place when they are young state troopers.

You might also see that much like our individual lives, there's an underlying force that somehow guides us to a point of meaning, whether we are in a position to discern it, or not. For me, I agree with Jack Patten when he says, "It's a God thing."

The Farm represents the fifth effort for Brooks Becker to copyedit, and for Stewart Williams to perform interior and cover design for my books. As always, they've done great work, and for their fine skills I'm grateful. And I'm especially thankful to Dan and Maurie Kirwin for having agreed to be my readers and critics—their comments proved thoughtful and insightful, and they inspired me to further refine the stories you're about to read.

What will you get out of *The Farm?* A comforting sense of hope, perhaps? A good laugh or two? A pause to make you wonder…?

Contents

The Farm

Much of this story came to me in a dream. Almost immediately, I wrote it down, and it still haunts me. One bit I added is a cameo appearance by Pennsylvania State Police Detectives Strand and Bentsen, lead characters in the Award-winning novels Winter's Dead and The Bitter End, as well as Murder Down Deep.

I was on the run from a troubled past, and it was looking like I was heading for a troubled future. A serious crime had been committed, and I felt responsible, but I did not stick around to face it. So, I ran.

Just to set the stage for what I'm about to tell you, the death occurred in late August 1977, in a college town in eastern Pennsylvania. Remember that year? Jimmy Carter had begun his first and only term, the Son of Sam killer had finally been arrested, and the Yankees and the Dodgers were headed to the World Series. But where I was headed was nowhere, it seemed. Where I wound up was a few miles beyond the little burg of West Middlesex on the other side of the state, where a lot of Amish families mix in with what they call us "English" folks.

What happened in between is pretty simple. I grabbed some clothes, jumped in my old Toyota Corolla, and got out of town as fast as I could make it that hot summer morning. After driving a hundred miles, I traded my clunker for another one, a 1969 Ford Fairlane, a blue two-door, and drove still further west. Every mile gripping the wheel, I imagined the Pennsylvania State Police on my tail, like my conscience chasing a guilty act. And when I saw a Trooper parked on I-80, I got off at the first exit and stuck to the back roads, always going west, away from what had happened.

Every time I glanced at my skinned and bruised hands as they piloted the old Ford, I was reminded of what I must have done. How could a night of pizza, beer, and a bunch of guys having a few laughs have gone so wrong? I hadn't wanted to be there. The two nights before with Angie wore me out, especially after we fought about the eternal question—was I ever going to settle down with her, or what?

Getting married was the last thing on my mind. I had no job and wasn't looking for one. Money had never been a problem for me because my parents always saw to it that I had plenty. My problem, I was soon to discover, was myself. Knowing who I was never hit the top three on my priority list. Fun was first, usually accompanied by a case of Yuengling, and, of course, my girl, Angie. Without a clue about the future, I was drifting from grad courses in history to nothing in particular, and my once-generous parents began asking me the same question that Angie was attempting to hammer home.

"Isn't it about time you figured some things out for yourself?" Angie demanded more than once. Angie and my parents. Two more reasons to run?

My parents, Warner and Doris, always had busy lives, and truth be told, I never really fit into their schedule. Mostly, I was an occasional entry in their daily planner. Later on, I'm guessing they suspected I was more about fun and games than books and coursework, and naturally, they were right. Without much guidance from them, I took the easy path—always. In their circles, I'm pretty sure people brushed off offspring like me with, "Oh, just let him find himself." That synced up well with W&D's *modus operandi.* And why face life if I didn't have to?

Running had been the first and only thing that came to mind when I woke up and saw the carnage around me. Could I have been so drunk?

Anyway, a fake ID helped me with the car trades, so I thought I was safe, but I could never be sure. A little bit of cash was what I had left over, so I had to be careful. My friends, the Yuenglings, would have to wait.

And so, I was twenty-two when I hit the town of Chance, PA, that Saturday morning, population 359 according to the sign. Ford pickups and Amish buggies dominated the two-block main drag, if you can call it that.

Up to this point, I suppose my story sounds like any other young-man-finds-himself novel, but at Corky's

Diner, smack in the middle of High Street, things began to take a surprising turn. Long and not very deep, the corrugated aluminum rectangle was the kind of place where, if you were sitting at the counter, you could see into the kitchen down to my left, and to my right, the other end of the place lined by booths and a few tables.

An older woman whose name tag said "Rosalee" asked me what I wanted, and after ordering their famous breaded perch sandwich—that's what the sign said—complete with tartar sauce and a few fries, along with a Coke, I just enjoyed the feeling of the place. Moms and Pops, clearly not society's upper crust, came in for Corky's basted eggs, home fries, and well-done bacon for $1.29. A few truck drivers camped on the round, red leatherette counter seats, like me. Most of us wanted our coffee, a task Corky's wife, Evelyn, completed while Rosalee took and served orders.

I might interject here that when I came in a few times afterwards, a girl about my age waited on me—her name was Emily. I learned that she was single, and maybe, just maybe, she was somebody I could ask out. For me, Angie was a past tense drama, and so, I had no romantic baggage to carry. I'm getting ahead of myself, I know, but Emily seemed a dream come true. She was pleasant, efficient, and drop-dead gorgeous.

Anyway, as I was finishing my sandwich that first day, Rosalee asked if I needed anything else, and that's when I asked her if anyone in town rented rooms. She eyed me curiously, thinking a moment, and finally said, "Let me ask Evelyn—she knows what's what around here."

In another few minutes, Evelyn stood behind the counter and gave me the once-over, too. "Who needs a room?"

"Oh, just me, ma'am."

"Got a job?"

"Not yet, but I have some money saved," I lied, "so I can pay the rent while I figure out what I want to do."

Evelyn nodded. "This is a small town, you know, but there are a few places you can check—I'll write them down for you. Otherwise," she paused for a long moment, "there's only the Whisp farm about a mile or so out of town."

"The Whisp farm?"

"Elmer and Agnes Whisp. They've had a boarder or two over the years. Don't know about now, though."

I nodded my appreciation, paid my bill, and climbed off the stool to leave.

"Don't expect much, young man," Evelyn said. "Only ordinary people live in Chance."

I couldn't have known it then, but later, I realized that when I walked into Corky's, I'd stepped into another world.

~

It didn't take long to find out that neither the Harshaws at the end of High Street nor the Steigerwalds on 2nd Avenue had anything for me, and so, with some disappointment, I climbed into the '69 Ford and followed the road out of town. At about the half-mile point, I slowed down when I saw an older man in a frayed straw hat working an ancient

John Deere. Seeing me wave at him, he drove the tractor over to the fence. When I asked him about the Whisps, he smiled and said, "You're in the right place, son. Just a bit further. Turn in at the mail box with the sign."

I nodded and said my thanks. It was a hot, humid day, and I could see the old man's temples were wet with perspiration.

"Don't be put off by the look of the place. Elmer and Aggie Whisp are awfully nice folks."

Once again, I nodded, and got back into my car for the remaining distance. In a few seconds, the wind began to stir up clouds of dry soil. Odd, I thought, given how wet the summer had been. And the old farmer I'd just seen was working a field of rich, dark soil, the kind that gave off an earthy aroma hard to forget.

Just at the half-mile point, as the dust cloud enveloped nearly everything around me, I came across a rusting, faded black mailbox somehow attached to a post that was part of a sagging fence line. The sign saying "Room" was nailed to the top fence rail. It was one of those white metal ones with a black border and black lettering, and it struck me that someone had just cleaned off what grime might have been there. Compared to the fence and the mailbox, it could have been new.

Glancing up the dirt lane, the billowing dust gave way to a surprising view. I noticed that the ground remained un-plowed, not ready for growing anything. In fact, the ground was practically a brown powder, the color of the creamed coffees I saw at Corky's, and remains of the previous year's corn stalks poked themselves above the surface. At the moment, this was no working farm, but hey, what did I know?

Up the treeless lane, I drove the Ford, quickly layered in dust, and in a hundred yards or so, I pulled up to a dilapidated house, its clapboards devoid of paint, its windows covered with the same dusty patina as my car. When I looked closer, I could see that someone had slapped some paint on one wall, but never finished the job. The front porch sagged at the corner, and didn't even seem safe to walk on. This couldn't be the place. But it was.

Yet, I needed a room, and the Whisp farm, such as it was, was my last chance in Chance. Carefully, I stepped onto the lopsided porch and made my way to the front door, the top half of which was glass, and behind which hung a curtain of some sort. I turned around and quickly calculated how long it would take me to get to my car in case this was the beginning of some wacko horror movie. But then the door creaked open, and facing me stood an eighty-odd-year-old man, stooped a bit, in faded denim coveralls. His plaid shirt had seen better days, as had the whiskers on his ancient face.

"Can I do somethin' for you, young fella?" His voice needed oiling as badly as the door hinges.

"Are you Mr. Whisp? Mr. Elmer Whisp?"

"Indeed I am, son. So what's on your mind?"

"I heard in town you folks might have a room to rent."

Mr. Whisp looked over his shoulder. "Maw, you better come."

Into the frame shuffled a woman of the same age, much

worn with hard work. She didn't suffer from hunger, plump as she was, and she wore a patterned dress that reached below her knees. Her old-fashioned pince nez glasses were smeared a bit, and her pure white hair was swept into a bun behind her head. When I glanced down at her feet, she wore the same black shoes as my grandmother, but the smile on her face was more welcoming than any I'd seen lately.

"We do have a room, son. Back of the house it is, and you'll have to share the bathroom with Elmer and me. Want to have a look?"

"S-sure," I said, not sure at all, and stepped through the door as they moved aside to let me in. Given what I saw of the outside of the house, I felt certain the inside would be as worn or worse, but I couldn't have been more wrong. The kitchen into which I stepped was as neat and clean as it could be. The Whisps took care of what they had. The big black cast iron stove in the room's center, with its exhaust bent into the wall, was something I'd only seen in movies like *Sergeant York*. There was a calendar on the wall but much of the print had faded out. I should have known, then, that the Whisp farm was somehow different from any place I'd ever been, or ever would.

Otherwise, the floor boards were covered with a green linoleum the color of seaweed. I was standing in a space that served as their kitchen, eating area, and sitting area. Plain but comfortable. The house was warm, too warm for my liking, but I followed Mrs. Whisp straight across the room to a door in the corner. No AC here!

"Here's what we have for you. It's not much," Mrs.

Whisp said, "but if you aren't too fussy, it's yours for ten dollars a day, and that includes meals."

"Ten dollars," I said, my voice louder than I intended it to be.

"Is that too much?" Mr. Whisp asked, bending forward out of concern.

"No. No, that's not too much at all." I was expecting it to be more, but since I had only about eighty dollars to my name, the price was good news. The room measured about ten by twelve with two windows looking out into the yard. There was no closet, only a few pegs on the wall that would have to do. Between two twin beds was a night stand with a candle soldered with melted wax to a tin pan. I turned to look at Mrs. Whisp, a question in my eyes.

"We have no electricity, you see," Mrs. Whisp pointed out. "It just hasn't come to us yet."

I nodded, not believing I had walked into this scene from yesterday. I'd heard that in parts of Pennsylvania and Southern Ohio, the remnants of an Appalachian time few people in the mid-seventies knew, there were still homes with cold water pumps and outdoor plumbing. Here was one of them. At least, she said, there was a bath of some sort, which seemed to imply hot water. Or so I hoped. As if reading my mind, she completed the thought.

"When it's time for a bath, we heat the water on the stove. It's a bit of work, but there's not much else to do on a Saturday night," she said, a broad smile decorating her face.

I nodded again, not at all sure I wanted to stay with the Whisps. Somebody around Chance had to have a room with 1977 conveniences. Right? But I didn't have time to look around, so I suggested that I take the room for a few nights, just to see how it went. It was a stay that lasted longer than I could have imagined.

The expressions on the Whisps' faces told me I'd made their day. Ten dollars wasn't much, but it seemed enough for them. "Let me get my things out of the car, then, and I can get settled."

They beamed.

~

By now you're wondering why I never called my folks, and you might have guessed the reason. We'd never been close, and once I went away to school, the distance grew. I was a total day care kid from infancy up to the day before my first day in kindergarten. When I became older, I sometimes thought I was just another ornament in my parents' richly textured lives. They had everything. Two houses. BMWs. A full-time housekeeper. And me. Only me. No pets. Neither my mom nor my dad wanted to clean up any pet messes, and the housekeeper said pets were not part of her deal. Sometimes it occurred to me that I wasn't part of the deal, either.

A dinner with my parents was a fairly rare occasion. They were always out with clients or at some charity event at dinner time, so it was Alice, the housekeeper, and me for dinner. Except that Alice had her own home and a husband waiting. When I was older and dinner time came, she put a plate down in front of me and made for the door.

If all that sounds strange to you, there were four or five kids in my class who lived in the same netherworld of family life. There really wasn't any "family life," if you know what I mean. Oh, my parents were generous with clothes and toys, and birthdays and Christmases were bonanzas, but even all the goodies grew tiresome. To top it off, we lived in a neighborhood of five-acre estates, so it wasn't as if a bunch of us kids were lucky enough to play stickball in the streets or anything like that.

Elmer and Agnes Whisp—he called her Aggie—were parents, but not like mine, that's for sure. They told me about their two sons, William Oliver and Lester Theodore, the second of whom went to war with the Marines but never came home. They didn't talk about them too much, but when they recounted their childhood antics, I could see the joy in their eyes. Their Marine son must have been a hard one to raise, from what they said, but they were very proud of him, I could see. And they missed him.

Decorations of any kind were few in the room or on the tan-colored plaster walls. On one, strangely enough, was a yellowing picture of Calvin Coolidge, and on another hung a photo of Lester Whisp standing tall in his Marine uniform.

I was surprised about the Coolidge picture, and my first night there after supper as we washed the few dishes in their galvanized metal sink, I asked Elmer about it. But before I get to that, I should note that my supper was a surprise in two ways. First, we bowed our heads in prayer, one which Elmer led. It was simple and short, but it was a ritual totally unfamiliar to me. Oh, I had learned about God, some generic, ethereal being who ran the whole show, but the Whisps taught me, over the course of my short stay, about another God, a loving and forgiving Being. Often, after dinner, Elmer would pick up their Bible and read quietly to himself, and on a few occasions, he and Agnes would involve me in a spirited discussion about good and evil, notions I never heard much about at home, or in college. And morals? That was an abstract concept to be memorized for a grade in a sophomore philosophy class, nothing more.

Back to the Coolidge picture. "Oh, we loved Mr. Coolidge," Agnes said before he could answer, "because he always encouraged hard work and independence. He was a very popular man."

"You wouldn't know that," Elmer interjected, lighting his corncob pipe as he did so, balancing the open Bible on his lap. "When FDR got in, they made a lot of fun of old Cal, but he was a mighty fine man to get us through the twenties." When conversation faded, they gave motion to their rockers, and I could see that they enjoyed the silence in the glow of the wood-burner.

Often, we talked about world events and American history—which pleased me as that was my own favorite topic—and I was amazed at the Whisps' thorough grasp of events about America's founding, and especially the Bill of Rights, a document they were fond of discussing. Their common-sense insights kept drawing me to them like a puppy to warm milk.

~

As you might suspect, I stayed with the Whisps more than the two nights I had originally planned. After supper on the second evening, I got up the nerve to ask them.

"You know, Mr. and Mrs. Whisp, I think I like it here, but I'm kinda short on cash to stay too much longer, unless, of course, you'd let me do some work around here in trade for my room and board." I couldn't believe I was practically begging them for a room. Me, the only son of wealthy parents! In a place with no electric, no radio, no TV. And no air conditioning! But I got the words out, and I could see small smiles break out on their ancient faces.

"That would be fine, son," Elmer began. "But what kind of work did you have in mind to do?"

I cleared my throat and tried to choose my words so as not to offend them. "Well, sir, I noticed that your porch could use some work—it's getting to the point where it might not be safe for you—in fact, it's sagging quite a bit."

Mrs. Whisp nodded. "He's right about that, El. You've been meaning to get at that for ages."

"Oh, and I could straighten some things out in the barn, too," I volunteered. The Whisps had let me put my car in what must be a hundred-year-old building, and I quickly saw it could use some shoring up.

Elmer Whisp nodded and smiled, his pipe glowing in the kitchen's waning light.

There followed a moment or two of complete silence among the three of us, and finally, when Mrs. Whisp broke it with a remark I might have expected, but caught me by surprise. I thought it would be a question.

"You know, Jack, El and I have been on this farm a while now, and have seen some tough times, but it seems to me you're going through some tough times of your own." She wasn't prying, but wanted to let me know she and Mr. Whisp understood something about me.

How did she know that? Looking down at the seaweed-green linoleum, gleaming even in the shadows cast by the light of the oil lamp on the table, I nodded. "I suppose you're right about that, Mrs. Whisp, but I'm not sure what I should tell you at this point."

"That's alright, son," Elmer Whisp said. "Whenever you want to talk about it, we're here. Seems it's just why we're here sometimes." He closed his eyes as if he was thinking about what he'd just said.

And that night, that's all there was. I thanked them for a good meal and went to my room.

~

The small room's two beds were generously called twins, but they were narrow ones at that, each with a thin mattress—I tried them both—resting on a set of creaking box springs that registered every move I made. Were these old Army surplus cots? From what war? As I lay there, a slim silvery light slipping into one window's edge, I tried to get out of my mind just what it was I didn't tell the Whisps.

I felt the knuckles of my hands. The once raw skin had

mostly healed over and the bruising was gone, but I'd seen Mrs. Whisp looking at them more than once. She didn't ask about them, and if she did? Then what? Would I have made up some lie to two people who were being so kind to me?

Sleep didn't come with the moonlight. Dozing was what I would call it, until sometime around sunrise.

I woke up to Mr. Whisp gently tapping at my door. "Up and at 'em, son. The missus has some bacon and eggs ready for us." The smell of frying bacon always reminded me of a Norman Rockwell cover on the *Saturday Evening Post*. There must be something in our genetic makeup that the smell of bacon evokes thoughts of sunny mornings in an old-time kitchen—at home. When I thought about it later, I found myself in that kitchen, but as for the home part, that—up until I came to the farm—I could only have imagined. I trundled myself to the Maplewood table that served as the center of the Whisp home, and there on my plate rested two eggs, sunny side up, and three strips of well-done bacon. "Mrs. Whisp," I ventured, "I notice there's a film on the eggs, like a mist in front of a sunrise."

"My, that's poetic, Jack," she said, laughing. "I make them basted, which means that when they're on the skillet, I cover them for a minute. El says that one little thing makes them the best eggs he's ever tasted, and I thought you would like them that way, too." I remembered one of my fellow diners at Corky's talking about his basted eggs— must be a thing for some people.

While she was talking, I used my fork and a piece of fresh-made bread to scoop up part of an egg, and once I savored the perfect taste, she could see the smile broaden my face—and her morning.

Mr. Whisp looked up from his plate and smiled—pure satisfaction painted itself on the nooks and crannies of the old man's face. "What's it gonna be this morning, Jack?"

"The porch, I think. Do you have a car jack around?"

"In the barn. You should find all you need right there— near our old car."

I hadn't noticed another car when I pulled my own in the darkening structure, but then I was just happy to have a place to put myself and my aging Ford for a little while. Mrs. Whisp brushed me away when I stood to clear the table.

"Just get at what you're going to do, young man, and leave my kitchen to me," she said with a gentle smile. "Elmer will stay and keep me company."

"Yell out if you need a hand," Elmer said, staying seated, basking in the warmth of the morning sun, his Bible near at hand, as always.

It was just at that point I noticed something was seriously missing from this scene. A dog lying by the stove. There was no sign of either a dog, or a cat for the mice, but I hadn't seen any of the latter, in the cleanest of clean old houses I'd ever been in. What farm didn't have a dog?

~

As I approached the barn—like the house with its paint having been bleached off by time and weather—I could see that whatever moisture had ever been in the wood had long since evaporated. Yet, I thought that if I had enough time, painting the house and barn would be a wonderful gift I could leave for them. But there was no way. These two rickety artifacts from another time would drink the paint like a camel after a trek in the desert, and the paint color would never show.

Anyway, I swung open the one big door on hinges that, surprisingly, still seemed sturdy and sound. Inside, my car already had a nice coating of dust, making it seem like the old Ford had been there for years. Mine wasn't the only old set of wheels there, I soon discovered, when I looked around and saw an undefined mound of something under a tattered gray tarp, soiled with age and speckled with straw and bird droppings.

I needed to find the jack, and Elmer said it was over by the car, so I began my search. To my utter amazement, what appeared when I jerked part of the tarp from the hood of what Elmer later told me was a 1932 Ford Coupe, complete with a rumble seat. The car's black finish, though a bit dusty, was pristine, and when I peaked in the driver side window, I saw shiny brown leather accented by the bright brass and nickel fittings of the car's controls, such as they were. In a minute, I found the jack in the Coupe's boot and set to work gathering a few other tools and what stout pieces of lumber I could find.

You're probably wondering how a kid like me became Mister Fixit. The simple answer is that through my high school years, when something broke around the house, it was left to me to figure out how to repair whatever it was. My busy parents had no clue. And sweet old Alice? No way. I stayed away from electrical and plumbing stuff, but otherwise, I gave it my best, and in the process, absorbed a bit of know-how.

Soon the sun was highlighting the front of the Whisps' farmhouse, ramshackle on the outside though it was, and I could see clearly that I had my work cut out for me. After a bit of trial and error, I was able to set the jack in the right spot so that I could lift one end of the covered porch without destroying the rest of it. I couldn't find a carpenter's level, and so I had to eyeball the amount of sag at the porch's outer corner. At first, when I pumped the jack I heard the groans of wood unused to movement of any kind, and perhaps, signaling an impending disaster. I decided to raise the structure only a fraction of an inch every half hour or so. That seemed to ease the old frame's pain.

At each change in the porch floor's position in relation to the earth, I stepped back fifteen or twenty feet to see what progress I'd made. By mid-morning, I was nearly there, and Elmer stepped out of the door and nearly fell over, unused to the floor's approximately level state. He'd been so used to placing his feet on a slope, he almost lost his dignity. "Oh my Lord," he called out as he grabbed hold of the doorjamb.

"It's okay, Elmer," I called back, forgetting to address him properly.

He chuckled, managing to clasp his pipe in his teeth as he did so, and said, "That's alright, son, I guess you're already making yourself useful here."

"Not really, sir," I said attempting to recover my error.

"You can call me by name, Jack. No harm in it, I suppose," he added stepping off the porch and checking out my work. "Hmmm! If I'd only have known a few hours work would have done the trick." He puffed on his corncob. "Interesting how just the right kind of effort makes all the difference, isn't it?"

With the sun in my eyes, I nodded. "Yessir," I said, and fleetingly, I considered all the lost hours in my short life. Into the gap between the original stack of bricks and the porch's supporting beams, I inserted two more courses and a piece of wood cut to fit.

Elmer had already gone back into the house, but as I finished up, I thought about what he'd said, because, honestly, I couldn't recall when I made a difference in anyone's life before.

~

Supper was a bit of fried chicken, peas, and mashed potatoes, the aromas of which I could savor all afternoon. Coffee afterward was accompanied by two Toll House cookies, like my grandmother used to make, but because she went to a nursing home before I was ten, I hadn't had them in well over a decade.

As delicious as Agnes Whisp's dinners were, I relished our times together as we sat near the black cast-iron stove centering the room. When the air chilled on a few late-August evenings, it was left to Elmer to stoke what embers remained after all the cooking. When I looked closer, I saw that it was a Glenwood with round plates on top that could be lifted to add fuel, coal, or wood, and warming shelves on the side for breads or pies. It was an appliance used frequently and well by Agnes Whisp, I can tell you.

"You can stop calling me Mrs. Whisp, Jack," she said as she made herself comfortable in the solid maple rocker. Elmer had his own, an armless oak number, with a rattan seat that had a few tears in it. "And thank you for fixin' up that porch. I was thinkin' El would never get to it, but here you get it done in a day."

I smiled. "Thanks, Aggie," I said, trying it out, "but it was my pleasure, and the least I could do. Believe me, I'm glad it wasn't more difficult than it was."

"So, what's next on your list, Jack," Elmer asked, "uh, not that there has to be something, you know, but you seem the type that likes to fix things."

"Oh, I don't know, but I'm wondering what a little paint would do for the place."

"Oh, my, you're ambitious," Aggie said as she rocked slowly, rhythmically, a sly smile spreading across her aged face.

"I'm definitely not that. If you only knew," I laughed.

As Elmer blew out a cloud of blue-gray smoke from his pipe, he said, "I only know this country wasn't built by lazy people, son, and watching you this morning told me you're not one of the lazy ones. Maybe you just need a target in front of you to shoot at."

I'm sure I blushed. Had my parents, my friends, my

college mates and professors heard Elmer's words, they would have howled. Yet, I took in what he was saying to me. I always put in the hours for American history, and the words of our founders, and I put whatever sweat it took to get something done I had an interest in. It was just that for most of my life, nothing seemed to interest me.

As if reading my mind, Elmer said, "It's not exactly what we're talkin' about, but I've heard that Abraham Lincoln once said, 'You'll be as happy as you make up your mind to be.'" He looked right at me.

"I guess you're saying that whatever I put in something, that's what I'll get out of it."

"Not exactly," he said, nodding, "but close enough. There's a lot in life that Maw and I have not liked all that much, but doing what we had to sometimes made all the rest easier to do."

"You know," Agnes chimed in, "Teddy Roosevelt used to talk about the man in the arena, the man who in the center of things does what he thinks best, not minding the jeers from the crowd—those who weren't brave enough to jump into the arena themselves."

"What are you telling me, Aggie?"

"You're here, I expect, because something's bothering you about your past, and you have no notion about your future. You're standing outside the arena, not sure to jump in."

"I guess so," I answered, trying to absorb what she'd said.

"I've always thought that what Teddy meant was that only in that arena do the choices become clear enough to see what comes next," she added.

"For me, I wonder what does come next."

"We love havin' you here, Jack," Elmer said, adding his nickel, "but people who stop by with us don't stay long, so I suppose you'll be moving on soon enough."

"You want me to leave?"

"Nooosir," he hastened to say. "You leave when you're good 'n ready, but when you go, know which road to take is all I'm sayin'." A log in the stove's firebox crackled, and a tiny jet of wood smoke joined us in the room, now silent except for the whispers of breezes in the late-summer evening.

~

Our after-supper conversations sometimes went late into the night, the oil lamp's wick getting its exercise, and they were never boring or lecturing. Yet, the Whisps always seemed to know what was on my mind, and what to say about it. Many nights, I took their words to bed with me. Thoughts from Jefferson and Franklin, right up to Franklin Roosevelt. The Whisps said he was so terribly right when he told them fear itself was their greatest enemy, and that the country could pull itself out of the ditch if only they made up their minds to do it.

Interestingly, when we got talking about the sayings of famous presidents, I mentioned Harry Truman's "The Buck Stops Here," but I was met with two blank faces. In my mind, that piece of information somehow tied to the fact that electricity had not come their way yet. Why, none of their neighbors, the Kengors, the McKnights, the Kingerys, had it yet, the Whisps said, so it didn't seem to bother them one bit. It was just the way it was.

Out in the yard a day or so later, I decided to rake out some of the sod, though I don't know why. All it did was raise a cloud of dust in a place where it seemed as if there hadn't been much rain. It made me wonder, though. For our suppers, we had fresh vegetables accompanying deliciously cooked fresh meats, even though I noticed no livestock around and neither did I see a garden when I walked around to the back of the house. Yet, there they were on our plates every day. Cool milk was plentiful, but there were no cows in the barn. Where was all of this coming from?

Another odd thing was that I expected to see laundry flapping in the noonday breeze on a clothesline around back. There was a clothesline alright, but it hadn't been used in a while, yet Elmer and Agnes Whisp always seemed to have on fresh clothing. And there was something else.

The day after I arrived, I noticed a blue police car go by the house several times. The officer didn't come down the lane and there was no siren, but it struck me he was keeping an eye on the Whisp farm. Was I becoming paranoid?

So many things about the Whisps didn't add up, but for the first time in my young life, I felt at home with people who treated me like their son, and I just decided that for some of the questions I had about them, I wouldn't search too hard for answers.

Have you ever noticed that? When you think you love

someone, you don't look too thoughtfully for the things that don't quite fit. As for the Whisps, I suppose I was beginning to love two people I'd only just met. But how could that be?

~

A day later with the Whisps, I made good on my ridiculous offer to paint their house. Mind you, with the porch raised on the one end and with a number of other fixes around the place, the small farmhouse looked pretty solid, except that it didn't have one brush stroke of paint anywhere, except the small patch around the window on the building's front side. Elmer mentioned that they'd had enough time and money to paint it a glossy white many years earlier, but more recently, it hadn't been very high on their list.

"A glossy white?" I asked him.

"Yep. Maw liked it looking clean."

"In all this dirt and dust?" I wondered.

"It wasn't always this way, Jack. In the Coolidge and Hoover years, things were green and plentiful. We grew corn and beans, had a couple of cows, and a barn full of chickens. Then, the winds came, out west, and here, too— at least for some of us."

"That was at least forty years ago, right?"

Elmer looked at me as if he hadn't heard what I'd said.

When he didn't answer, I asked him, "What if I picked up a few buckets of glossy white and did it up?"

He chuckled. "It'll take more'n a few buckets, son. This

wood'll drink that paint like a thirsty dog on a hot July day."

Never had I heard him be so colorful. "Okay, you're probably right. Where can I get some paint in Chance?"

It took him only a second to say, "Why, at the Western Auto downtown, right next to the Ritz Theater. The man there knows us."

"A theater? I didn't see one when I was there."

"Oh," he chuckled, "the Ritz has only one center aisle with four seats on each side, and not twenty deep. Not a big building. Easy to miss." He chuckled.

~

Halfway into town in the Fairlane, I realized I didn't have much money for paint, brushes, and the like, but went ahead anyhow. Easily, I spied the Western Auto and found a parking space right in front. It didn't look too busy.

Inside, the air moved only because of the two ceiling fans, the front-most one operated by a long leather belt from the one in the rear. Elmer mentioned that the man to talk to here was his old grade school friend Fish Gilbert. "The tall one," he described him.

I saw him writing some notes at the counter in the rear, and introduced myself. "You the boy staying at the Whisps'?"

"Yes," I said, wondering how he would know that. "I'd like to get some paint for their place. Mrs. Whisp wants it white."

"I've known Aggie for a long time, and if she wants white, that's what she'll get. Probably gloss white."

I nodded. "You're Mr. Gilbert, aren't you? You know, I don't have much money. How much will it cost me to paint their place?"

"Hmmm. You'll need plenty of primer, brushes, pails, thinner, and our best Dutch Boy oil base—glossy, right?"

"I guess so. Aren't there water-based paints out now?"

Fish Gilbert looked at me strangely. "If so, they haven't hit Chance," he said with a laugh.

"And the cost, sir?"

"Oh, we'll put it on Elmer's tab, son. Don't you worry. Elmer and Agnes will be good for it."

It took him a half an hour or more to gather it all up and load the Fairlane's giant trunk. "Holy cats," he said, "I haven't seen a car like this one before."

"Really? It's a 1969 Ford Fairlane."

He just looked at me, and then over my shoulder, past me, nodding to someone in the near distance. I turned to see a man in a policeman's uniform leaning on the hood of his navy-blue patrol car, parked a few feet up from my own.

"There's Willo now. You met him?"

"Who?"

"Willo. Willo the Whisp," he said, smiling. "He's the Whisps' youngest son. That Elmer had a hell of a sense of humor when he named that boy!"

I looked the officer up and down, and his car, and to be sure, it was the same car that rolled past the farmhouse so often. Although I was scared out of my wits to be approaching a police officer, I crossed the few steps and introduced myself.

"And I'm staying with your folks," I said after giving him my name.

"Hmmm. I thought I saw someone around the place." He nodded, to himself, apparently. "I'm sure we'll talk again," he added, then turned and got into his car.

~

Painting the old house was a more daunting chore than I thought. First, I spent two full days priming two sides of the house. Elmer was right, of course. The dried-up wood soaked up the paint to such a degree that a few hours after I applied it, the white primer took on the appearance of a chalky gray. At that point, I knew this would not be an easy summertime gig, but the days were cooling, and it felt great to be working out of doors.

At one point at the end of the first day, just before dinner, Elmer and Agnes stepped out into the front yard, and shielding their eyes from the sun, nodded and smiled. Agnes was especially happy. "Jack, I'll make you the best apple pie you've ever tasted. This old house is becoming a treat for my eyes."

The woman's cheer and appreciation served to spur me on, and by the end of a week, I had the two sides primed and painted, the gleaming white a sharp contrast to the remaining two sides of the seemingly ageless building. When it had been built, Elmer did not know, and Agnes only guessed that it had been around since President McKinley's days in office.

To complete the new look, I washed and shined the windows—each with its original wavy panes. Agnes produced a can of window wax—something I'd never seen or heard of—and I can tell you the wax and elbow grease made all the difference. When I stood back to admire my work, I could easily have been tempted to forget about the rest of the place, but I knew that Agnes, and even Elmer, would stand a bit taller as masters of their bright and clean homestead.

All the while I was painting, taking advantage of the shade when I could, the older blue police car made its back and forth patrols. But Willo the Whisp, as Fish Gilbert called him, never stopped to check in on his folks.

Another full week passed, and after another umpteen gallons of primer and Dutch Boy paint later, the Whisp farm home practically glowed in the fading light the last Friday I was there.

~

Agnes Whisp outdid herself with a pot roast in a large pan with peeled and halved potatoes and a load of carrots. After she decorated a large serving platter with it all, she used the juices to make gravy with a few tablespoons of cornstarch. And then she served us the feast, coupled with homemade bread and butter. Did I mention the onions? It seemed that Agnes never made anything that went on the table before dessert if it didn't have onions, and to this day, I can bring back the taste of that day's supper with only a bit of concentrated thought. I won't mention the apple pie—my mouth would begin to water.

What I can also bring back was the gentle way in which Agnes prodded me to talk about that which I didn't want to talk about at all. Yet, her doing so didn't ruin the meal of meals. I might mention that I could never bring myself to call her Aggie again, because Elmer did so with such charm and affection I felt embarrassed to imitate. Agnes attached no strings to her questions, but asked them with a warmth of caring I could almost call love, that which a mother has for a son. I'd been there barely a month. How could she love me?

"You know, Jack, we all carry baggage in this life, things we wish we hadn't said, things we wish we hadn't done, but what Elmer and I have learned over our marriage is that forgiveness is often just a few words away."

When she said those words, hardly above a whisper, I put my fork down, and for what seemed a minute or so, I could only chew the last bits of beef teasing my taste buds. Finally, I lifted my head, took a deep breath, and began.

"I didn't think I'd ever want to talk about this with anyone," I said haltingly, "because I think I may have killed a man."

Elmer and Agnes sat stock still, their forks resting on their plates.

"A bunch of us had an apartment together off campus," I continued, my voice hoarse with reluctance and emotion both. "I'd finished my undergraduate degree—in history, if you're interested—and I stayed on for my master's mostly because I had nothing else to do." I stopped to gather my words a bit.

"The other three guys were a year behind me, and were waiting to begin their own graduate work. I had another semester to go before finishing my master's degree, and my roommates and I had no clue about our future lives. I had no job in mind. I just assumed some high school somewhere would hire me to teach history." I let out my air. "Anyway, one of the other guys said we should have a party. Hah. Didn't we always have one going?"

My listeners remained silent.

I licked my lips. "The beer and the booze were plentiful. It was a Friday night, just like this, only there was no real food in the picture. Chips, pretzels, dip, fried chicken, and beer, mostly beer. No girls. The more I drank, the more depressed I became, and the more morose my thoughts were, the more I drank. There was an argument going on that I wasn't part of, and I have no idea what it was about. Money, maybe? That's about all I really remember. At some point, I went into my room. My intent was to throw myself onto the unmade bed, but I didn't make it. I hit the floor, and that was that. Dimly, I heard the other guys getting louder and louder.

"The next morning I awoke with a headache like no other. I went to the bathroom and lost everything in my system—sorry to mention that—then I drank what seemed like a gallon of water and stumbled out into the living room, where I saw all the damage from the night before. Tables and chairs were upended. Food was everywhere and the place stank to high heaven. All I could think of was who was going to deal with the landlord about the mess.

"Then I saw him. Pat was on the floor, right up against the wall, his head at right angles to the rest of his body. As I looked closer, I could see his face bruised but pale, and on the wall just above his head, a splotch of blood. When I saw all that, I noticed my hands, raw and skinned at the knuckles. For a few seconds, I couldn't connect the dots between Pat's face and my hands."

I took a few deep breaths, but dared not to look directly at Elmer and Agnes. I didn't want to see what they were now thinking of the young man who just finished painting their house.

"And what did you do?" Agnes asked, kindly.

"First, I knelt down next to Pat and touched him. Through his T-shirt, I could feel that his body was cold. I called his name, poked him a little harder, but he didn't move. His chest was still. And I looked at my hands again and, and…" I stopped speaking. They waited for me. "And I began to cry because it looked to me that I did this to my friend, only I was too drunk to know it. I went all through college with Pat, and I killed him."

"Where were the other boys?" Elmer wanted to know.

"No one else was there. It was totally quiet. I sat on the floor next to Pat trying to sort things out, but nothing made sense."

"Your story doesn't make sense either, Jack," Agnes Whisp interrupted, her voice firm. "You're left handed. Surely, you didn't strike your friend with both hands?"

I looked right into her eyes. "You're right, Mrs. Whisp, but how did my hands get so scraped?"

"I can think of a dozen ways," Elmer said. "Maybe when you fell in your room?"

I sat, not moving, but concentrating. In my beer-infused haze, I could see myself falling, but missing the bed. The wooden bed rails. Of course, my knuckles smacked right into the bottom edge of the darn bed rails! "You might be right, Elmer. But what happened to Pat?"

"Perhaps," Agnes said, softly, "now would be a time to stop running and talk to the police."

I nodded. It made sense. But hearing her logic did not mean I could actually do it. Stop running? As if reading my mind, Elmer leaned forward and tapped my knee with the stem of his pipe.

"You know, son, if you keep running, you'll never really know what happened to your friend. Just knowing you these past weeks, I can't believe you'd pummel your friend, drunk or sober. Don't you want to find out?"

~

The sun seemed to rise earlier the next morning, as if to give me a head start on doing something I didn't have the courage to do. When I lifted my head from the pillow, there was something different about the house. I didn't hear any of the usual kitchen noises. I couldn't smell Agnes's coffee. It was very still. And it was chilly. Hadn't Elmer fired up the stove?

Shivering, I stood and threw a shirt and pants on, then stepped into the main room of the Whisps' world. There, too, nothing stirred. I stepped across the wooden floor and tapped lightly on their bedroom door, but there was no answer. Could they have gone to town? To tell the police about me?

I tapped again and called their names. When I heard nothing, I eased the door open. I had never invaded their privacy, and I didn't want to start now. In the morning light streaming through the room's one window, I could see Elmer and Agnes Whisp lying in bed, the covers up to their chins. But like Pat's, their chests didn't rise and fall with life's usual rhythm. I went over to the bed, but could see, immediately, that life had already left them.

With the deepest sadness, I knelt by the bed, next to where Agnes Whisp lay, and said the only prayer that came to me: "Eternal rest be unto them, O Lord, and let your perpetual light shine upon them." I couldn't stop the tears.

For some minutes, I remained there, thinking about the real parents God had given me, even for just the few weeks I'd known them. They'd given me hope, faith, and yes, even love.

I knew what I had to do, and within a few minutes, I made myself presentable and drove into Chance as fast as I could get there. In the same parking space a door or two away from the Western Auto store, there stood the old blue police cruiser with Chief Whisp leaning against the hood holding his morning cup of coffee. I could see the steam rising when I came close and said, "Chief, I don't know how to say this, but your folks died last night."

Willo the Whisp stood there not saying a word for several seconds. "I know they're gone, son."

"How could you possibly know? It just happened!" I saw an expression on his face I couldn't figure out.

"Son, my folks died in 1943, just a few days after they learned that my brother had been killed in the Pacific."

"What? That couldn't be. I just spent nearly a month with them!"

"Oh, I know you were at the house, because I saw you there, and you did a nice job with the paint and all, but you couldn't have been with my folks." He exhaled and took another sip of coffee. "Now, if you'll excuse me, it's time for me to go." He straightened his hat, climbed into the cruiser, and drove off with me standing there.

I looked around to find someone else on the street to talk to, but it was too early. No one was out and about, yet. When I turned in the other direction, I looked into the front windows of the Western Auto, but it was dark. In fact, the window displays were gone.

As I took a few steps further, I saw that the diner's sign was flashing its "Open" welcome, so I went there to find Emily, the waitress I met earlier.

Breathing a sigh of relief that she was there behind the counter, I sat down, asking for coffee as I did so. "The strangest thing just happened to me," I began, even though I really didn't know her well, only the few times I'd been in for breakfast. "That cop told me the old folks I'd been staying with died years ago. Can you believe it? Hey, where's

Rosalee—she's the one who told me about the Whisps in the first place."

"Good Lord, Jack, did you fall and hit your head or something? What cop are you talking about? This town's too small to have a policeman. And who's Rosalee?"

I grabbed onto the counter to make sure it was real. I stared into Emily's eyes to make sure she didn't think I was crazy, but I wasn't sure what I saw. Concern? Fear?

"Hey, why don't you talk to the two Troopers who come in every morning? They'll help you out." Her words were kind, but careful.

"Troopers?"

"Right. Little towns like ours don't have their own policemen anymore. The Pennsylvania State Police covers us. Their barracks is just up the road."

I nodded, barely comprehending what she was telling me, not to mention what I'd experienced in the past month. After she brought me my coffee, I sat there trying to sort it all out, when the two staties she mentioned came in and sat a few stools down from me. I shivered.

~

It took me a few minutes to get up the courage to say anything to the two uniformed men deep into their coffee and breakfast platters. Finally, I said, "Do you guys mind if I talk to you for a minute?"

The closest trooper to me was tall, fit, in his thirties, and carried a no-nonsense look about him. From what I could see of the other guy, he was even taller, beefier, and tough to the bone. I introduced myself, but at first neither of them gave me their names. "What can we do for you?" asked the Trooper closest to me while the other one tucked into his eggs and potatoes.

"I don't know how to start," I said, nearly choking on my own coffee. "I'm staying at the Whisp farm not far outside of town. Been there almost four weeks now, but this morning, when I woke up, I found Mr. and Mrs. Whisp d-dead in bed. I don't know what happened—they were fine last night—and when I came to town this morning and told their son, the Police Chief, about it, he just said, 'I know,' and drove off. I really need you guys to come out and take a look."

The Trooper furthest away, still chewing, piped up. "What Police Chief?"

"Why, the one they call Willo the Whisp."

"You know, my friend," he said turning to look right at me, "I'm from around here and everybody knew Willo when I was growing up."

"Then what's the problem?"

He cleared his throat. "Willo was killed in the line of duty some fifteen years ago—shot by some guy here in town—so, I don't know who you talked to, but it wasn't Willo!"

"God, who could it have been?"

"I don't know, Jack, but are you sure you aren't hungover or something?" asked the first Trooper.

"I haven't even had a beer in weeks, ever since…"

"Ever since what," the really big guy wanted to know.

"Do you guys have names?"

The first one said, "Trooper Strand, and this is Trooper Bentsen. Now, ever since what?"

"I'll tell you that later, but first somebody's gotta come out with me to the Whisps'."

"Let me finish these eggs," Bentsen said. "I'm guessing they'll still be dead, right?"

I winced.

"Sorry, I thought you'd only been with them a few weeks."

Nodding, I added, "That's right, but they meant a lot to me."

Two minutes later, Trooper Strand stood up, grabbed my bill, and paid Emily at the register. "C'mon, let's go. We'll drive."

~

In the Pennsylvania State Police Ford Explorer, specially modified, I noticed, they put me in the back seat and asked for directions. "Oh yeah, I know the place," Bentsen muttered. "Looks pretty run down."

"It is. Or was. That's what I've been doing to earn my keep with them. I didn't have much cash when I came here, and they were kind enough to let me work around the place for them."

"Where'd you come from, Jack?" It was Strand, who was driving.

"Eastern PA," I responded. "I can tell you about that, later."

In less than five minutes, we were turning down the lane to the Whisp farm. To me, it looked the same, but quiet and still.

"Nice paint job, my friend," Bentsen said, peering through the windshield.

"Thanks—least I could do. The place really needed it."

"Needs a lot more than that, I'm thinking," he continued. "Good God, look at this place. Hasn't been farmed for years. And the barn—pretty much falling down."

"Elmer Whisp has his car in there. You should see it. A '32 Ford Coupe, he told me, in mint condition."

Trooper Bentsen turned, giving me a quizzical stare.

Trooper Strand pulled up in front of the house and sat for a few seconds, taking it all in. "I'm surprised you stayed here, Jack—except for the paint job, the place looks abandoned."

"Not at all," I said. "Let's go in."

I was the first up the two steps onto the front porch I so carefully rebuilt, then into the front door like I owned the place. They followed, but a few steps in I stopped so suddenly, Trooper Bentsen bumped into me and almost knocked me down.

"What's the matter?" he asked and I could see his hand sliding over to his sidearm.

"Everything's changed. Some of their stuff is here, but it's dirty, dusty—Mrs. Whisp would never let her home be like this." I noticed Lester's Marine picture was gone, and the one of Calvin Coolidge was lying on the floor, its glass shattered. The door to my room was open, and, strangely, there was my bed, just like I left it, and what few things I had hanging on the wall or sitting on the dresser. "I can't figure this out. My stuff is here, but theirs isn't!"

Trooper Strand stepped around me and walked toward the only other door in the room. "This is their bedroom, I take it?"

"Y-yes," I said as he swung it open.

The Whisps' bed was there alright, but bare of sheets, blankets, or pillows. The room was completely empty, as if someone had left it years ago. Needless to say, Elmer and Agnes Whisp were not lying there in repose. They were no-where. The Troopers turned to look at me.

"Son, what are you up to?" It was Bentsen. "Looks like you've been squatting here on someone else's property."

"Of course not!" I protested. "If I was breaking the law, why would I find their son to tell them about it? Why would I approach you?"

Strand and Bentsen looked at each other. Then Trooper Strand said, "You said there was something else, something you would tell us later. Now would be a good time, Jack, be-cause it looks like you've been wasting ours."

I took a step back. Trooper Bentsen said, "You know, son, I think you should come with us to the barracks where we can have a nice chat. There's more you need to tell us, I'm thinking."

I didn't know what to say or do. I couldn't believe any of this. From their point of view, it was exactly what Bentsen said—I'd been using someone else's property to hide out.

After a few seconds, I looked at both of them. "I'm very confused right now, so I'll do whatever you want. But what about my car? And my stuff inside?"

"No one will bother anything, don't worry. If need be, we'll get your stuff for you," Strand said as he touched the back of my elbow to steer me back to the Explorer.

"What kind of car did you say was in here?" Bentsen asked, walking the few steps toward the barn.

"A '32 Ford, but at this point, I wouldn't bet on it."

"Guess not," he said with a smile I couldn't figure out.

Bentsen stepped into the barn and was out less than a minute later. "Nothin' there, Fletch."

Once again, they both eyed me carefully. Strand asked me to climb in the back seat of the Explorer, and we left the Whisp farm, I thought, maybe for good.

~

At the PSP's Mercer County barracks, the Troopers walked me into their one interrogation room. In a minute, a woman entered and said she needed to take down all my basic information. She said her name was Florence Moses.

I surrendered my driver's license—my real one—and my wallet. I was aware of people having credit cards, but I had nothing like that—who would give me credit?—and there was nothing else to identify me. She asked for any other addresses, and I gave her the one at college. "Do you want us to contact anyone? Your parents? Relatives?"

"Why would we need to do that?"

"Well, you never know," she said, not unkindly.

"No, I'm an only child, and I'm not close to my parents, so why bother them?"

"Okay. The Troopers will be back in a few minutes as soon as we check some things out."

Ms. Moses brought me a cup of coffee that came out of a reservoir of used motor oil. "Want a donut? We have a few left over."

"No, thanks, ma'am. I'm not feeling that hungry this morning."

She left without another word and I was alone, which is not always easy, but the seemingly endless minutes gave me some time to think about the Whisps. What they taught me over the few weeks I was with them was, well, priceless. They never gave me advice, and neither did they lecture or hector me for being the lost soul I made myself become. But they seemed to care for me, and I promised myself never to forget them.

Their gentle questions forced me to be honest with myself, to provide my own advice, and to kick myself in the butt for not having a clue about what I wanted to do in the world. No, not what I wanted to do, but how I planned to make myself useful to the world.

The door opened and Trooper Bentsen strolled in, followed by Trooper Strand. Just by the way they carried themselves and sat down opposite me across the gray linoleum-covered steel table, I sensed that my world, such as it was, was not going to end.

Strand said, "Well, we ran your driver's license

information across our card indexes, called our guys nearest your last residence, and did a name check with the FBI in Washington, and nothing. So, that's a good start."

"You mean the police aren't looking for me?"

Strand looked at me square in the eye. "Now do you want to tell us about it? What you referred to at the diner?"

I swallowed hard but thought about the Whisps, and what I owed to myself first of all. "I-I thought I hurt someone, maybe killed him, my roommate, Pat Mattey, back there."

"Keep talking," Trooper Bentsen said, making notes.

For the next few minutes, I spilled out the whole story, the whole weight of my conscience, with every detail I could remember, all the things I mentioned to Elmer and Agnes. The two listened carefully, and finally, Bentsen said, "Sit tight. I'm going to make a few more calls."

Meanwhile, I sat with Trooper Strand, and we became a bit more acquainted, but in less than five minutes, Florence Moses entered the room and asked Strand if she could sit with us.

"You know, Jack," she began, "I'm from around here. In fact, I grew up in West Middlesex, the next town over from Chance."

I looked at her expectantly, having no idea what she was about to tell me.

"I've heard a lot about the Whisp farm over the years, just stories, you know, but no real details. So, when the boys brought you in here, I decided to satisfy my own curiosity about them."

I could hardly breathe and could see that she held Strand's full attention.

"According to friends in this part of the county, I'm sorry to tell you, Jack, the Whisps died just before Christmas, 1943. Strangely, they died in their sleep, brokenhearted some said, when they learned their son died in battle just after the Marines landed in Tarawa that November. It took a few weeks for them to receive their telegram, but they were devastated."

"They died back then? How could they? I lived with them, ate with them, heard stories about their sons."

Ms. Moses shook her head. "I believe that you believe what you experienced, but…"

"Just a second. There was a picture of their son, the Marine, on the wall, right next to one of President Coolidge. How could I have seen that?"

"I don't know, Jack, but some folks around Chance say you're not the first person to have spent some time with the Whisps. Waiting for their son to come home, some say."

"But they had the other son, the one they called Willo."

"All the old ones around here said Elmer and Agnes doted on Lester, and they were so proud of him, they seemed to forget about Willo. Even so, Willo loved his folks, anyway, and looked out for them. Maybe that's why you met him."

"And what about the guy at Western Auto, Mr. Gilbert?"

She smiled. "Oh, the Western Auto closed years ago, so I don't know who or what you saw."

I shook my head. "But he gave me the paint Elmer

wanted for his house. Dutch Boy. That was real!"

"I can't explain it, Jack. Something happened to you in Chance, but…"

The door opened and again, Trooper Bentsen lumbered in. "The police department in your town knew all about the death of Patrick Mattey, and they have in custody the man—your age—who came in and confessed. They had a fight about who owed who some money, and your room-mate fell and hit his head. They're dealing with it. Your name never came up, except that you owe your landlord some rent money." When he finished, he just smiled, shook his head, and added, "Guilt can do some interesting things to people, you know."

Stunned. That's what I was. Stunned. What happened back there wasn't what I thought at all. The fact was that I was a lazy guy who didn't give a damn about anything, but kill somebody? No. You have no idea how relieved I was to hear what Trooper Bentsen had to report, but at the same time, I was ashamed of myself for running, for taking the easy way out.

But what about everything that Mrs. Moses told me? I still don't fully understand what happened to me, but things sometimes work out, don't they? Had I stayed put in eastern PA, I would never have met the Whisps.

"You're free to go, Jack," Strand said after a minute or so. "We'll drop you back at your car, but you know what? I'd move on, if I were you."

～

I asked the Troopers to drop me off at the diner. Working up new courage, I decided to stop by to see if anything might go forward with Emily. I know I had stars in my eyes, but if I learned anything from Elmer and Agnes Whisp, I had nothing to lose by asking.

At the counter, I ordered a Coke and a grilled cheese sandwich when I saw that Emily was there and smiling when she saw me. "So, I guess you're not on your way to the slammer, huh?!"

"Not this week, anyhow. Hey, I was wondering if you'd like to catch something at the Ritz."

She started laughing so hard, she almost spilled my soda. "The Ritz? You mean Chance's one and only form of entertainment? The one that closed before the moon landing?" She continued to laugh and, of course, I turned three shades of red.

"Sorry," I stammered. "I thought it was still open. And if I asked you out to eat, I'd have two problems."

"Which would be?" Her eyes sparkled.

"I have no money, and if I did, I'd have to take you here!"

Emily laughed but said, "You know what, Jack, I'd love to go out with you, but I don't think you're quite ready for me. Would you promise to come back when you have some idea what's in front of you?"

I let all my air out. "That's the nicest letdown I've ever heard."

"No letdown, silly boy," she said and leaned over the counter to plant a kiss on my cheek. "I just want to be surer about you being sure about me. Now, get outta here, and get started with something—then come back. I'll be waiting."

~

I had a lot to think about on the mile ride out of town to the Whisp farm. You can guess, by now, that I didn't encounter the old guy on the John Deere. When I arrived at the farm, I knew what I had to do next. For now, though, I savored the special moment I had with a pretty girl I sure wanted to see again. But when could that be?

I had a few things still inside the now glistening white farmhouse, and even if Elmer and Agnes weren't there, I needed to go get my stuff. Nothing had changed, of course, since early that morning, but I admit being just a bit apprehensive about walking into a house where I was absolutely certain I'd seen two dead people just hours earlier.

As I stepped across the threshold, however, there was something different yet again. To my mind, the place seemed tidier, and it didn't smell of dust and forgotten memories. The Whisps' bedroom was still pretty much empty, but mine wasn't. I packed what there was that I could call my own and sat on the bed staring out the window at the empty fields.

At what point I laid my head back and closed my eyes for a bit, I have no idea, but I did not awaken until the next dawn—to the smell of breakfast in the making. I could almost imagine Elmer tapping on my door and saying, "Up and at 'em, Jack. Aggie's got some mighty good bacon on the skillet."

The aroma of frying bacon was there, alright, but no one or nothing else. I washed up a bit, grabbed my stuff, and walked out the front door, but not before taking a good look around the place. It was then that I spotted the dust-covered book resting on a small table near the Glenwood stove. It was the old family Bible, and as I thumbed the worn pages, I came across a piece of folded paper tucked in right at the 23rd Psalm. When I unfolded it and saw what it was, I replaced it where the Whisps had apparently wanted it to be, and carefully returned the Bible to its resting place.

What was the piece of paper? It was the telegram. Elmer and Agnes Whisp had been waiting for their son, but all they had of him was a War Department telegram announcing his heroic death at the altar of freedom.

I took a deep breath, climbed into the Ford, and drove to the top of the lane. Before I turned onto the highway, I stopped, got out, and using a towel from under my seat, I shined up the black and white metal sign that said "Room." A sudden swirl of dust bid me goodbye.

At that moment, I could easily imagine Elmer and Agnes welcoming another lost soul someday soon. And you can easily imagine my smile as I drove away to face a future I hadn't thought I had.

EPILOGUE

You'll want to know the end of the story, I suppose. The Jack Patten you met in 1977 did, indeed, find his way—right after finishing his degree and returning to Western

Pennsylvania, but to another town not far from Chance, where he taught high school Civics before retiring thirty-five years later. He and Emily Klein married, had four children, and lived happily ever after. And yes, the Pattens prayed before meals and went to church every Sunday, and often enough, they extended their own welcome to lost ones they met along the way. Jack once explained to his children that the most important fact he ever learned in life was that someone not of this world is looking out for them. "It's a God thing," he said.

Their lives weren't perfect, however. While the Pattens enjoyed a broad and filling family life, it was without his parents. Once, on a short visit, he overheard his mother tell his father their son's life turned out to be "so ordinary." His mother's judgment sealed the fate of their relationship, and that was fine with him. They never saw each other again.

Early in their years together, Emily helped Jack find the final resting places of Elmer and Agnes Whisp. Their marker showed the same date of death for them in 1943, just as Florence Moses—and Chief Whisp—had said, about twenty-four years before Jack met them. As far as they could tell, the Whisps had no living relatives. At least once a year, they placed a bouquet of flowers on their graves, and early on, they were surprised to find that others had been there to leave bouquets of love and remembrance before them.

Growing Up with Lady of Spain

This is an autobiographical tale, one with which some readers will be humorously—or painfully—familiar.

We all have memories we'd rather not relive, yet all of them shaped us, right? This story is a slice of when I was a cocky teenager in the early 1960's, a time when I learned too much about myself. Embarrassment was one feeling I had navigating that passage in my life, and in one of the episodes I'm about to relate, it turned out that I did it all to myself. That I can laugh about all of it now may be a testament to any maturity I may have attained in the meantime, but none of it seemed so funny then.

Let's start at the beginning, where all the real trouble began.

Growing up in Buffalo, New York, in Cheektowaga to be

exact, I was the second son in a family so thoroughly Polish, our veins had no blood, just bits of Cabbage Pierogi floating around to confound the medicos unfortunate enough to treat us. Like so many other families after the war, my father wanted something better for us—a 1950s version of The American Dream. For them, it was a hard pull at times. Neither of my grandfathers could read or write, and what formal learning my parents had obtained was, shall I say, basic. Despite their Great Depression beginnings in large blue-collar families, Ed and Irene struggled to make their dream happen. Like your parents, no doubt.

And so, when I was about seven or eight, my parents decided that one way of showing a successful migration up the rungs of the social ladder was to have a child who could play a musical instrument. I have no idea who put so crazy a notion into their heads, but instead of focusing on my older brother who was busy delivering *The Buffalo Evening News* every day after school, they chose me to represent the family's musical prowess, even though no one in two generations had been known to play anything except a phonograph.

When they asked me what instrument I wanted to play, I could only see hard work ahead and lost time away from my pals. I didn't like the prospects one bit. On wavy-screen black-and-white televisions in those days, everybody watched Lawrence Welk or Ed Sullivan. And let us not forget Liberace! In my clever little brain, I looked around our modest home on Shanley Street and I finally relented. "I want to learn the piano!"

Ed and Irene were honest with me: "We can't afford a piano, and we have no place to put one, anyway." I sighed with relief, as you can imagine, and smiled inwardly, toasting my victory with a glass of Nestle's chocolate milk,

A week later, however, after we were forced to watch still another of the weekly Welk extravaganzas (remember the Lennon Sisters?) my parents said, practically in unison, "Look at that Myron Floren with his accordion!"

Lying on the floor, eyes keyed to the flickering screen in front of me, I paid no attention.

"Phil!"

"What about it?"

"That's what you'll learn to play!"

The accordion?

"Think of it," they said, "you can play at family parties. Your grandparents will be so proud." Disaster loomed. Too surprised to cry, I just whined for as long as I could get away with it. Myron Floren might be one talented guy, but I wanted nothing to do with the accordion. There was to be no reprieve.

~

The next thing I knew, they marched me into Walt Struba's Music Center on Clinton Street (I have no idea if his name was Walt Struba, but let's let that go for now), and soon, he was showing me the indented C key on the left side of the giant squeezebox thrown into my lap, and then the scale on the piano-like keyboard on the right. "It's easy," he said.

Right! That I was left-handed seemed not to matter to Struba or my parents. I guess there were no left-handed accordions. They were hell-bent on finding something to keep me busy and out of their hair. All smiles, they were.

I might point out here a genetic flaw I must surely possess. Have you ever noticed kids who are naturally coordinated? They grace athletic fields with their muscularly articulated presences. And kids who excel athletically also seem to do well with music. Have you ever noticed that? For me, not so much. So, it wasn't just that I was lazy about the accordion's requirements—and I was. It was also true—I came to learn—I had NO natural abilities with music or, for that matter, a few other worthwhile activities.

In a few weeks, my very own accordion arrived, one which my loving parents bought on the installment plan. It was a silvery-gray marbleized number—you've seen them, for a while they made kitchen table tops that looked the same—and for me, it weighed a ton, but made a nice first impression on sweet old ladies, especially those hard of hearing.

Worse than being enrolled in this school of horror, I learned that my parents weren't going to drive me to those Friday night lessons, either. Oh, no. I was going to have to walk the million city blocks to Mr. Struba's Chamber of Horrors right near the Strand Theater—lugging along the instrument of said torture. Okay, maybe it was only six or seven city blocks, but, sun or snow, I struggled with the Silver Beast. And I wasn't a big kid! Why couldn't we have lived the American Dream with a harmonica?

Did I mention that I hardly ever practiced on the darn thing? Yes, I went week after week, subjecting myself to the trudge—walking back and forth lugging that monstrosity and changing hands every few minutes, not to mention listening to Mr. Struba telling me over and over how I had to practice more.

"You'll never be like Myron Floren," he said to me more than once.

"That okay by me," I said.

"But you'll make your mother so happy," he said, "and maybe one day, you'll be on TV!"

"Not on your life, Mr. Struba."

Well, he was almost right, but I couldn't see that far into the future.

~

I always wondered why Mr. Struba wore earmuffs—he said he was cold, but I suspected even then it was not the reason for him to plant them on his shiny bald head as soon as I walked through the door, and began to demonstrate my "progress" for the week.

Mr. Struba was patient, but never seemed to hear me say that I hated the accordion and never practiced, anyway. Instead, he encouraged me and my parents to continue with this evil, at least as long as the weekly lesson and installment dollars kept coming.

Naturally, I told my parents Mr. Struba said that I was so good, I didn't need to practice songs like the Morris

Dance and Five Foot Two, Eyes of Blue, not to mention the Beer Barrel Polka, the Clarinet Polka, and Nola, as well as a half a dozen Christmas carols. If I did fifteen minutes some days, I must have been sick with something or otherwise so bored, I could think of nothing else to do.

My friends Petie, Paul, and Mikey all learned how to play baseball as I did, but none of their parents had the same musical aspirations for their sons, I guess. Or at least, their dreams did not involve Myron Floren. A couple of times, I invited the gang to walk to the lessons with me, but when they found out that really meant helping me carry the silvery plastic monstrosity in its brown leatherette case a million blocks, their interest faded to zero. I also think they didn't want to be seen with anyone who was weighed down with, of all things, an accordion. A bat or ball autographed by the Buffalo Bisons was one thing, but an accordion? No way!

The Lawrence Welk Show was a staple in the otherwise barren B&W television desert, and it seemed to be the only show my parents watched with my grandparents. Every time Myron Floren was showcased, I was obliged to pay the closest attention to, and admire his fancy fingerwork on, you guessed it, his gleaming black and white instrument. He was supposed to be my hero. And here I thought it was supposed to be the Yankees' Phil Rizzuto, Whitey Ford, or naturally, Mickey Mantle!

~

The months of agony did not speed by, but my upper arm muscles bulked me up, an odd image for a kid going from eight to ten years old in a blink. Even a keyboard bum like me learned how to stumble through a few tunes, much to the chagrin of many.

Each Christmastime, for instance, when the whole gang of my extended family gathered at my grandparents' home on Meadowbrook Boulevard, I was forced to drag along the great silver beast to play "Silent Night," "Noel," "White Christmas," and so many others that I know my aunts and uncles, despite their frozen smiles, wished for a truly silent night once I began playing. The cousins I thought were my lifelong buds sat in the corner and howled. And do you have any idea how many times I had to play "Happy Birthday" as a special treat to some unsuspecting soul?

And then something happened that I thought would change everything—at least as it involved the accordion.

My father came home one day in the spring of 1958 and said he'd been transferred to the brand-new Ford plant in Lorain, Ohio, and so we were moving beyond the edge of all living things. As painful as that was for an eleven-year-old, the silver lining, to me, anyway, meant saying goodbye forever to Mr. Struba and the Friday night accordion torture.

So, that July, we settled in Huron, Ohio, a nice little town nestled right along Lake Erie's southern shore, nearly midway between Cleveland and Toledo. What a new life it was. From the industrial, urban setting in Buffalo, we found ourselves in a beautiful beach town, and life was good, I thought, especially with no accordion to hug every day. I buried it in the closet. Oh, what a foolish boy I was!

~

Living in Huron meant going to watch the Indians or the Browns play, swimming off sandy beaches all summer long, going to Cedar Point pretty often—only five miles away—and enjoying all the things small-town living had to offer. Opie may have had Mayberry, but I was lucky to be in Huron.

Summer slipped into fall, and I was happily enrolled in St. Peters Elementary School, surrounded for the first time by twenty some other kids I didn't know. I was the new kid with the long Polish name nobody could pronounce, much less spell. The nuns were good, though, and the days passed happily. Huron was so small, however, it didn't have the one thing my parents were unreasonably passionate about—some poor soul who would give accordion lessons to their beloved second son. In that knowledge, I was comfortably smug, but like all kids, I underestimated my parents' persistence.

With only one car in the family, planning was everything. My mom insisted that my dad take us to Sandusky every Friday night after dinner for a round of shopping. What else? The big A&P store there was the draw (remember The Great Atlantic & Pacific Tea Company?), and I should have expressed my enjoyment pushing the grocery cart, but how was I to know what was to come?

Ed and Irene had evidently heard that a Mr. Larry Fortunato had a music store in the same plaza (what we now call a strip mall) as the A&P, and there he held forth as the local virtuoso of you guessed it, the accordion. Truly amazing, wasn't it? And yes, he had an opening on Friday evenings when my parents could do their grocery shopping. How could accordion lightning strike me twice? The poor soul had no idea what was coming—and neither did I.

"Mom and Dad," I said one day, "I don't know whether you've noticed, but I H.A.T.E. the accordion and everything about it."

"But you won't have to carry the case anymore, Phil, because we'll take you."

"How convenient!"

Mr. Fortunato promised my parents great things if they just put their precious boy—and the Silver Beast—in his capable hands. Of course, that would take hard work and practice on my part, he said, but I had no intention of changing my lazy ways when it came to pounding those notes. Little League and new friends at St. Peter's School were my sole interests.

But who was I but a lump of clay—or mud—in Mr. Fortunato's hands? So, week after week we went. The same routine. It sucked. They loved it. And while I progressed in my feeble abilities on the right hand piano keyboard and, less so, on the left-hand button board, Myron Floren had no worries.

Week after week, while my mom was raiding the A&P

shelves, I was lying to Mr. Fortunato about how much I practiced on the great silvery beast half as big as me. The good man was patient, but soon, he too caught cold and donned earmuffs when I showed up for my thirty-minute lesson every Friday at 6:30 p.m.

~

In Ohio, at least, few relatives would be around at Christmas, so I didn't have to worry about another holiday session of horrors in the carol department. However, Ed and Irene, a lot of fun mostly, found me an audience. They had developed a good circle of friends, who, despite the requirement that they listen to me play holiday tunes, continued their relationships with them. It never bothered me that even when I pounded out old favorites at yuletide, some of them would ask, "What song was that?" Sing-alongs helped, but only if they sang louder than I played.

Thus far in my career as an unsuccessful purveyor of strange squawks coming from an otherwise fine instrument—Mr. Fortunato made sure I knew that on several occasions—I managed to get away with minimal time with that thing strapped to my shoulders, claiming it would ruin my posture for all time, but no one believed me.

All the time I plotted and pleaded to forego the Friday night evil—I wanted to be at the Huron High School's stadium watching our Tigers do their best, after all—I suppose, looking back on it, Mr. Fortunato must have been planning his escape, too. The great silver beast as well as the earmuffs were getting to him, I suppose, but I could never have imagined what would come next.

My parents continued to watch Lawrence Welk—and made me watch, too—so that I might be inspired by the inestimable Mr. Floren. But I was not interested, and by the time I went to high school, another interest compelled my attention: a short parade of pretty girls who for whatever reason found me appealing.

My high school physics lab partner, Jane, and I soon became an item, one to last through our high school years, and as an added bonus, she and her parents lived only a few blocks away from us. With no car at my disposal, I became a welcome visitor at her parents' home. Naturally, they were aware of the weekly torments my parents put me through with the silver squeezebox, but expressed no interest in hearing me play, and neither did I encourage that notion.

To any other sixteen-year-old kid, Easter 1963 would be a welcome spring holiday, even if not for religious reasons. Growing up on what some people came to call "The North Coast" was a lot of fun for most of my peers in Huron, Ohio, but that particular year, after Mr. Fortunato's great news, it was going to turn out to be the great comeuppance—for me, that is.

It would have been in late February, probably, that Mr. Fortunato announced to my parents that he had a special relationship with the manager of the local radio station, WLEC AM&FM ("1420 on your AM dial"). And lucky for me, he said, I was to have the opportunity of playing my accordion, live, on the radio that April. My parents, naïve souls, were astounded, thrilled. "But," Mr. Fortunato said, "you're really going to have to practice, Philip! You'll be playing 'Lady of Spain' and 'Easter Parade.'"

Unfortunately, all my friends' families could pick up the WLEC signal. Can you imagine anything worse?

~

Play on the radio? Live? On the air? There was no way out, save an alien landing from another planet where accordions were outlawed. A radio performance might be viewed as pretty cool by some people, but not me. How could I not foresee the consequences of years of keyboard neglect! So dumb was I that I mentioned the forthcoming radio show and coming infamy to my girlfriend and her parents, and, naturally, my parents were equally foolish enough to tell their friends as well.

My date with destiny was going to be the Sunday before Easter that year. "Lady of Spain" was a real challenge piece and "Easter Parade" was a favorite for the season written by Irving Berlin. Do I need to say a few things? My parents were beside themselves that their little Phil was going to play on the radio. I stayed true to my lazy nature and practiced little—I suppose I hoped the "Think Method" espoused by Professor Harold Hill in *The Music Man* would see me through. My greater mistake was to remind my girlfriend and her parents to be sure to listen to WLEC around 11:30 a.m. that Sunday.

Because the radio station itself was no bigger than a

large bedroom, divided into a teeny lobby and a small studio, my parents had to stay in the car listening to the radio broadcast from the parking lot. Good thing. For me, the sheer terror of realizing the "Think Method" was not going to do the job struck home as I dragged the accordion case, a music stand, and the sheet music into the fateful venue.

There I sat in the tiny studio, fumbling with my music stand and the sheet music for two heretofore great tunes. Mr. Fortunato was nowhere to be found, because either he couldn't fit into the room, lost his earmuffs, or was on his way out of the country. Surely, he had to have known what was coming.

One saving grace was that the announcer so tortured my nine-letter Polish surname that it was likely only a few people knew it was me. He pointed at me through the glass in the control room, and I began "Lady of Spain." Needless to say, it was an abysmal rendition of an otherwise tuneful piece. The announcer wanted to shrink away, no doubt, but had nowhere to go. Then came what I did to Irving Berlin's "Easter Parade." I'm sure my off-key rendition didn't remind anyone of Easter or Judy Garland's version of it.

I had kicked over the music stand after the first few notes of "Lady," but in a few minutes, it was all over. In my ego-driven teenaged mind, I convinced myself I'd done, well, okay. How delusional could a teenaged boy be? I couldn't hear anything the announcer had said, but he was smiling as he pointed me to the exit, and out I went, dragging my music and the great silvery beast.

Back in the car, my parents said, gamely, how "nice" that was, but said little more except that one of the perks of Mr. Fortunato's arrangement with WLEC was that they were to have a 45rpm record of the entire performance as a treasured keepsake. My girlfriend and her parents were kind enough to pretend they'd forgotten to tune in for my six minutes of radio infamy, and though my feelings were hurt a bit, in truth, I felt relieved. Jane's father capped off the whole sorry mess by mentioning that "Lady of Spain" was the signature piece of, yes, you guessed it: Myron Floren.

~

When the day came that the 45rpm record arrived in the mail, my parents insisted that we all listen to it together on the big stereo in our living room—did you have one of those? Six feet long with speakers at either end, an AM/FM radio and a record player built in? Despite the slaughter of our surname, the announcer's voice came through the speakers with quite a nice intro before I began to play. Suddenly, I couldn't breathe. Could the violent noises coming through the speakers be me torturing my accordion? After I finished "Lady of Spain," and then "Easter Parade," the announcer said, "Wow! Irving Berlin would never believe he wrote that one."

Although he was hearing it a second time, my father chuckled, and my mother covered a smile with her hand. When the needle slid to the center of the record, I said,

"Don't you two think it's time I moved on to something else?"

"Why?" they asked, a grin on their faces I cannot describe.

"I don't want to compete with Myron Floren," I said. Don't get me wrong, I love accordion music and still listen to polkas on Pandora, but fast fingers on two keyboards were never going to be me.

The announcer's parting line stayed in my head until a few years later when I understood his double meaning. Fortunately for radio listeners everywhere, I did find other pursuits—girls for one, and no, that 45rpm record no longer exists. Bye-bye, Myron Floren!

~

My years at Huron High School proved an awakening for me in other ways. Despite outstanding teachers, I performed at a mediocre level—remember I said that an inveterate laziness was my driving force in those days? Oh, there was Mr. Richards in Algebra, Miss McKillip in Latin, Miss Windau in English, and best of all, Mr. Klein in Civics, a course of interest that has stayed with me to this day. I earned top marks in his class, but in few others.

Demonstrating to Mr. Struba, Mr. Fortunato, and my parents, not to mention WLEC's many thousands of listeners, that I had no talent or interest in playing a musical instrument was one thing. Another was my lackluster ability on the wrestling mats under Coach Ford's tireless tutelage. I was the problem, not him, of course. After earning my Reserve Letter, I decided athletic contests were also not the arenas for me.

For most kids, high school activities allowed them to discover what they were good at. For me, I learned what I needed to stay away from. Music and athletics were two, but there was one more lesson in store for me.

An even more public embarrassment was about to come my way when Mr. Adler let the Sword of Damocles fall on my head, in a manner of speaking, of course. Much beloved by many, Mr. Adler taught English and was responsible for putting on and directing all the school plays. I did not have him in class, and until one winter day, I had never spoken to him. For whatever reason the Fates made clear to him, he approached me and told me I was to be the lead character in his next school play, *Cloud Seven* by Max Wilk, a drama recently on Broadway.

What? Had everyone else turned him down? The poor soul hadn't heard me on WLEC, but had he done so, my future in the footlights might have remained a mystery. But, no!

~

Recently, I looked up *Cloud Seven* and found that it was not Max Wilk's best effort. Far from it, according to a *Time* magazine review from that era. In brief, here's the storyline for the play:

In this late 1950s comedy, Newton Reece—played by

the hapless Ralph Meeker on Broadway and, later, by the equally hapless me at HHS—is a thirty-nine-year-old, married commuter, a rising star at United Foods, who cannot find himself doing what he's supposed to be doing to support his wife. He tries everything, often blasting away at his trumpet to while away lazy afternoons not going in to work.

You get the idea. Apparently, the play bombed in New York, and I helped it bomb in Huron. One has to suspect Mr. Adler bought the rights to put it on for the loose change in his pocket. Then he needed an idiot to play Newton Reece. That's where I came in.

High-schoolers did not say no to teachers way back when, and even though I was wary of so flattering a demand of my unknown skills, my parents insisted that I do what Mr. Adler asked. There was a catch. Isn't there, always?

Did I mention that the play's lead character had to play the trumpet? If I didn't play the accordion, I sure had no acquaintance with the trumpet, right? I told Mr. Adler so.

"You know music, Phil, so this will be easy."

Me? Music? "Mr. Adler," I pleaded, "you don't know this, but at St. Peter's the nuns always asked me to just move my lips during song time. And besides, I don't even have a trumpet, and truth be told, Mr. Adler, I'm lousy with an accordion."

"You'll have to play only a few notes," he said, ignoring my every word. "Even an idiot can do that." Now you know why out of 400 kids, he chose me.

"But what about the trumpet part?"

"I'll fix that," he vowed.

Next thing I know, my good friend George entered the picture. George played the trumpet in the marching band and earned side money as the projectionist at the Ritz Theater [yes, the one described in *The Farm*], and was a great guy to hang around with, not to mention getting free admission to the Ritz's projection booth. Anyway, George agreed to teach me how to play the trumpet in two easy lessons. He lent me his instrument and showed me the basics.

"You'll have to practice on this, Phil!" George admonished me. Well, you know how that went, don't you? My cheeks hurt, my lips bled, and I still couldn't make a sound any different than the blatting of Foghorn Leghorn. My parents had sympathy for me, and dug out their earmuffs.

"I can't do it, Mr. Adler!"

"Wait right here." You've never seen a man so exasperated. He didn't swear at me, but turned several shades of red, steamed up his glasses, and seemed to turn his blond crewcut a ghostly shade.

In a few minutes, he returned with another of my friends from the band, Jon, a fellow wise guy like me and a year behind George and me in school. George's evening projectionist duties made him unavailable for this gig, if you want to know. Naively, I assumed that Jon would replace me as Newton Reece. As John Belushi famously said so many years later, "But, nooooo!"

"Jon will stand in the wings and play your notes as you stand in front of the curtain at the scene opener, and for the two other short occasions Reece grabs his trumpet. All you have to do is mime the whole thing."

"Mime?"

"Yes, pretend to play."

"Why doesn't Jon just play Newton Reece for real?"

"Because you're the guy, Phil. Now, get to work with Jon, and it'll be just fine."

Well, we did practice this bit several times, while otherwise kidding around. Yet, it went well, and as opening night loomed, I felt confident we could pull it off.

Fate had its way with me again that Friday night when *Cloud Seven* opened to a so-so house, a small consoling fact to me later. Just to set the tone of Reece as a guy who is mournfully lost, Reece appears in front of the curtain—no scenery—and blasts out six or seven notes on a gleaming trumpet while the curtain opens behind him to his New York City apartment.

I stepped through the curtain's center cut and stood there as the house lights went down on the audience and a spotlight came up on me. Glancing to the off-stage right position, I saw Jon standing there at the ready. Raising the trumpet to my lips, I began to mime my act, but Jon just stood there laughing his head off.

Me, ad-libbing as best I could, took the trumpet down from my face, and repeated the start-up gesture, and again, no sound poured forth from George's trumpet. Jon laughed. Mr. Adler walked up behind him, fuming. The audience, now on to the fakery we were attempting to pull on them, just howled.

What could I do but lower the trumpet again and laugh with them as Mr. Adler chewed Jon out, unheard over the audience's laughter.

Had there been a voice-over announcer, he might have said, "Max Wilk would never believe he wrote that!"

~

The spring of 1963 wasn't all bad for me. Although I'd learned that sports and I weren't going to be best friends, that I couldn't get by playing an instrument, and that I couldn't act, there was a tiny light in the darkness that I should mention.

Did I forget another great teacher? In junior year English class with Mrs. Janice Browne, we were tasked to write a short piece of our choosing, for a grade, of course. Mine was called "On Happiness," and I thought I'd just hand it in and that would be that. It didn't work out that way. Mrs. Browne called on a few of us to read our pieces aloud. I shrank in my seat. To no avail.

Did I mention I was not much of a student the first two years in school? I was a wise guy who fooled around most days. It was my friendship with Jane, our class ace and ultimately our valedictorian, that brought me to my senses. Did you have someone like that in your young life? Because of her, I put extra effort into everything, including assignments by Mrs. Browne, who called on me to read.

Unused to anything serious from me, my classmates were, shall I say, dumbfounded when I read "On Happiness." Mrs. Browne remained silent for a moment, too. "You wrote that, Phil?"

"Yes," I said, and she said, "Please see me after class." Uh-oh.

When everyone was gone, she asked me her question again. And again, I replied in the affirmative. I'd written it myself, had no help from anyone. She gave me an A. Before I left, she said, "Someday, Phil, you ought to think about writing more seriously."

Many may agree that I need more practice at it, but thank you, Mrs. Browne, wherever you are.

Eddie Novak

This piece is pure fiction, here because I wanted to explore the notions of sin and redemption, as well as the downsides of revenge.

A h, you came, Father!" The man's voice was raspy, hurried. "I need to tell you about a guy who killed people, then killed himself. At least, that's what everybody said." His eyes darted as he rattled out the words. "His name was Eddie. Eddie Novak."

Father Michael Pallison had just walked into the hospital room, but it was as if he had walked into the middle of a conversation. He waited. In a hospital setting, heavily medicated patients were often the rule, and he had learned to expect almost anything.

The man in bed laughed at himself, the wrinkles around his mouth stretching in both pleasure and pain. "S-sorry, Father—just anxious to tell you the story."

A hearty man, Pallison gave the patient a chuckle of his

own. "So who is Eddie, and why would you be wanting to tell me his story, Mr. Koski?"

"It's Jerry, Father, and his name is Eddie Novak. Did I say that? I put myself on the list so you would stop." Jerry adjusted the blanket, concentrating on his bony fingers, and trying to hide his fear that the one man to whom he could tell his tale might not return.

"Not a problem," Pallison mumbled in a half-formed grin. Koski could never have been a tall man, the priest surmised—maybe 5'8" at best, but now capped by a smear of wispy white hair stuck to a discolored, peeling scalp. Eyes that might have once been blue now appeared a foggy gray with just a trace of sky.

"I'm not from around here, by the way, and if you were wondering, I haven't been to Mass in quite a few years." Jerry surveyed the younger man a few feet from him. With dark hair framing shaded skin, this guy is what they call Black Irish, he thought. Warming to the priest's smile, he concluded the man had a sense of humor. He hoped God did, too.

The priest nodded. "So, you wanted to see me?" he nudged.

"Yeah. I'm guessin' you come around once a week or so, and I was hopin' you'd find time for me."

"Sure, Jerry." Pallison paused to form his words more carefully. "So, you think you'll be in here for a while, then?"

"They're runnin' a buncha tests, Father. They think it's cancer, but they're not sayin'. Probably pancreas."

"Sorry to hear it, Mr. Koski," Pallison said. "I hope it's not the case."

"Yeah, well, it is what it is. They told me it might take a few days or so before they have a plan worked out."

"That long?" It was not a question. "Too bad you have to wait."

"Well, maybe they're stallin' a bit because I don't have anybody, and they know the news ain't gonna be that good, anyway."

"Perhaps you should be a bit more optimistic, Mister, uh, I'm sorry, Jerry. Here at the Clinic, they can do almost anything."

Jerry nodded. "Save it, Father. I'm pretty sure what's up. That's why I wanted to see you. They said you were a good listener."

"Thanks—practically all I do sometimes."

"That's all I want—that is, if you have the time."

"Not a lot today, Jerry, but I'll be glad to come back.

"You're not from around here?"

"No. The other end of the diocese."

"Ah. Eddie wasn't from here either. We met not long before he died." Jerry stopped there, remembering.

"And…?" Despite the bravado, Pallison knew he'd have to prompt him. People with a death sentence, real or not, always seemed to be partly in another place.

"Eddie would want me to tell his story—I'm pretty sure I'm the only one who knows it, and you're the only person I should tell it to."

"Whatever you say."

"Well, it all started in 1973."

"You mean twenty-five years ago?"

"Yeah, that long ago. To me, it was like yesterday." Koski let his gaze pass through the large hospital window and wander into time's distance. "You remember the early seventies, Father?"

Pallison could see the happier memories pink up Jerry's cheeks. "Yes, I do, in fact. I'd been out of the seminary for about ten years." The priest chuckled. "Let's see, wasn't Nixon president then?"

"You got it. And by the end of the year, Spiro Agnew was gone and Ford was in. Remember that?"

"I do. For me, 1973 was another kind of milestone. The Vietnam War was ending and then, there was Roe v Wade." The priest did not smile then, and added nothing to his simple statement.

With a nod, Jerry acknowledged the priest's words. "*Kojak* was on TV, and so was *M*A*S*H*," he went on, keeping away from subjects dealing with life.

"And gas was what, thirty cents a gallon? Jerry. Back to Eddie?"

"Sorry, Father, it's just that there were some good things about those years—before they weren't so good." The light went out of his eyes. "Eddie told me that was when it all went bad for him, too."

"What happened?"

"He began to kill people. At first, he felt good about it, but then he didn't want to stop. He thought he would get that good feeling all over again, but it didn't turn out that way."

"I don't understand."

"You see, Father, the first guy Eddie killed was for revenge. Because of what the guy had done to Eddie's family when he was a kid."

"Eddie told you all of this?"

He nodded.

"You have my attention. So, what happened to his family?"

"It was in the summer of '58. July. In New York—one of the boroughs, but don't ask me which one it woulda been—I have no idea. His pop had gotten a new car the year before, a '57 Ford Fairlane, a Tutone Tudor—Ford's clever way of saying two-tone, two door. Yeah!" he continued. "He even told me the colors: snowshoe white over buckskin brown."

Pallison waited, astonished yet puzzled.

"The family was set to move to Ohio, where there were some relatives in a little town near Cedar Point—you know, the park with all the roley coasters. Anyway, they were packin' up the car after the truck left with their stuff. That's when they came."

"Who?"

"Two guys pulled up in a black Buick—they got out of the car and went up to his folks as they were carryin' cardboard boxes out to the car. Somethin' was said, and they all went into the house. Eddie said he could never forget that day…"

"Where was he?"

"He was next door having a goodbye lunch with his best

friend—they were having tuna sandwiches in the side yard. And remember, Father, nobody had air back then and New York woulda been stinkin' hot, so all the windows were open. Eddie could hear stuff breakin'—glass, mostly—and loud voices. You could hear everything, he said."

The priest could almost see Jerry gathering his thoughts from the dusty shelves of memory. They seemed to give him strength. Whose memories were they…?

"Anybody else around?"

"His sister, Rosie, was inside. She was a few years younger than Eddie, maybe six or seven. The two guys were accusin' Eddie's father of holdin' out on 'em, like he owed money or stole it."

"Was that true?"

"Eddie says not. I guess Novak is a pretty common Slovak name, and there were a buncha Novaks in his neighborhood, some of them related, but most, not. Later, he did some diggin', and it couldna been Eddie's father they wanted."

"Okay."

"Eddie listened outside the window. From the sound of it, the two thugs were beatin' up the old man pretty good. His mom was yellin' that there was some mistake, but they kept at it. They said his old man was gonna leave town with the money, but his father said it was not him, somebody else. He could hear Rosie bawlin'.

"Mr. Novak was cryin' and beggin' at the same time. Eddie said he wanted to run in and do somethin' but it was like his Keds were nailed to the ground and he stood there not able to catch his breath. So the beatin' went on for a while, and suddenly, it stopped."

"Just like that?"

"You remember those toy guns that used to shoot ping pong balls?"

"C'mon, Jerry, what are you talking about? Yeah, I remember them—had one myself, in fact. So?"

"Eddie said it was as if somebody shot three ping pong balls—there were three soft pops, and everything was quiet."

Both men became silent, until Pallison broke the moment. "And then?"

"Nothing. Eddie was so scared he couldn't move. The two guys couldn't see him, but Eddie could see them. They got in their car, and took off.

"When they left, Eddie started screamin' his head off, and some neighbor women came runnin'. Two women ran up to him and asked what was the matter. He told them somethin' bad happened in the house.

"The women ran in, Eddie behind them—they tried to stop him, but it was too late. Eddie saw everything. His pop was a bloody pulp, and all three had been shot once in the head—even Rosie. It was a mess."

"Oh my God! That poor kid. His sister too?" The priest was stunned—this was not a "confession" he'd ever encountered before.

"Yeah. I guess they thought she was old enough to say what she saw."

The priest inhaled deeply, then let out his breath. He didn't need to say anything.

"Well, for Eddie, that was that. The police showed up, of course, but nothin' came of it. It was a mob thing, it turned out. The cops probably knew that and just assumed Eddie's father got his. Not a lot of sympathy there, you know."

"Oh, c'mon, Jerry, not when they killed the missus and his sister! Nobody killed kids back then."

"Maybe. You'd think those murders woulda been easy to solve, but they never were—at least, by the cops."

"What do you mean?"

"First, it got worse for him. Not only did Eddie lose his family, all their stuff disappeared too. And when it was all over, nobody stepped up to take him."

"Not even the relatives from Ohio?"

"Nobody."

"So what happened? You said he was only eight?"

"Orphanage. Then foster homes. Finally, the Ohio people adopted him. But he was never right, and he never forgot about what had happened to his folks and Rosie."

"You're keeping me in suspense, Jerry. Then what?"

"Eddie grew up messed up. You can imagine what worked on this kid's head for all those years as he was tossed from one place to another. And the guilt, Father. Eddie convinced himself that if only he had run back to call the police, if only he had run into the house, if only this, if only that."

"Guilt can really do a job on some people. I hear about it every week in the confessional."

"Finally," Jerry went on, like a jukebox that had played the record many times before, "in early 1973, when he was

about twenty-three, Eddie was back in New York lookin'
for a job, and one day, while checkin' the *Post* help-wanted
ads, he noticed an article about a murder trial where the
guy got off. That started him thinking about things.

"Next, a friend of a friend pulled a string or two and got
him a maintenance job with the NYPD. It didn't take Eddie long to figure out where the old records were kept. Once
he was assigned to the right building, like that"—the feeble
snap of the man's fingers produced no sound—"he's into
the cold case boxes down in the basement."

"So it was Eddie's plan to get on with the PD?"

"Mostly dumb luck, Father. Haven't you ever noticed?
Most people would never commit a crime without the
right set of circumstances coming together right in front
of them."

"Maybe. But no set of circumstances makes anyone
commit a crime, Jerry."

After a few seconds, Jerry nodded. "Whatever you say."

Pallison took in the words along with the curious tone.
"Back to the old files. Anything in them?"

"Nah! Except one of the cops seemed pretty sure who
actually did the work."

"And it went nowhere?"

"Pretty much. Squeezed in there were the notes from
one of the detectives. There was a name underlined three
or four times—that's where the notes ended."

"Wait a minute. Are you telling me Eddie could recite
all these details from memory?"

"Yep. Amazing what comes out after a week huggin' a

bar! And after a lot of beer."

"Where was that?"

"Oh, that was in Huron, where Eddie wound up. That's where we met."

"Boy, am I confused. New York, Ohio—you've got a lot of blanks to fill in."

Jerry chuckled. "All in good time, Father. All in good time." As he said the words, his smile disappeared as he wondered just how much more time he had. He guessed the same thought crossed his visitor's mind as well.

"I've got just another minute, so let's end a chapter of this if we can."

"Not interested, Father?"

"Oh, I'm interested, Jerry. You tell a good story, and I'll be back next week, but there are other sheep in the fold, you know."

Jerry laughed out loud. "Sheep! Sure. Just remember, Father, it's not just a story."

Pallison nodded. "You were saying—there was a name?"

"Oh, yeah. Sam Zirelli—one and the same guy whose picture was in the paper. Can you beat that?"

"Never heard of Zirelli. Who was he?"

"No reason you would have. And 'was' is right! Zirelli was a low-level underboss for one of the borough families, and he's been dead a long time."

"How do you know that?"

"Because he was the first guy Eddie killed."

The absolute certainty of Jerry's words stole Pallison's breath. He rose. "Okay. I'll be back. I hope things go your way. See ya, Jerry. And by the way, it's Mike." Pallison made the sign of the cross over him.

"Okay, Mike. Stay tuned, as they say."

~

"Hi, Jerry. I see you moved. How're you doing?"

"Oh, so-so."

"Good thing you left a trail—I wasn't sure what was up when I saw the empty bed."

"Hah! I knew you'd want to hear more about Eddie."

"That too." The priest inhaled deeply, a simple act giving him time to form his next words. "The fact that you're here in hospice tells me something else, I suppose."

"Yeah. Like I told you, the docs were pretty sure what it was, but they wanted to see if there was something they could do."

"And?"

"No luck, Mike. No treatments, no trials. No nothin'."

Pallison touched Jerry's arm.

"Not much time left." Jerry cast his eyes downward. "It's just as well."

"I don't like to hear that kind of talk, Jerry. Let God decide that for you."

Jerry did not acknowledge what the priest had said. "Where were we with Eddie?"

"Wait a sec, Jerry. How're you doing with," he gestured with his hand, taking in the place and circumstance, "everything?"

"How can I be doing with it, Mike! Like I said last week, it is what it is. That's why I have to tell this story. Now." Jerry stayed silent for a moment, letting the finality sink in with his visitor.

"Okay. I get it. So tell me, then. Eddie murdered this Zirelli guy. How did that all come down?"

"Let's see," said Jerry, happy on his mission, "did I mention Eddie's maintenance job with the PD? On top of him having access to the old records on the night shift, he had his days free."

"For?"

"For stalking Sam Zirelli. Over a period of three or four weeks, he tailed the guy three or four days a week, and none of his goons ever noticed. Anyway, it didn't take him long to see that the guy had one particular pattern. He went to the same restaurant every Wednesday at 5:30—somewhere on the edge of Little Italy, Luigi's Pizzeria."

"He went to a pizza place?"

"Yeah. Apparently, a lot of those dumpy little places, holes in the wall really, had back rooms that served really good food. Now, if that's where Zirelli met his guys or what, I don't know because Eddie never said."

"Wait a minute, Jerry. You missed a few pieces. You said last week that Zirelli's name was in the detective's notes, but how did Eddie know for sure that this guy was somehow responsible for the murders of his parents and little sister?"

Like a traffic cop, Jerry held up his hand to stop the flow of words. "Are you some kinda detective yourself, Mike? Here's all I know. Remember, Eddie wasn't married or anything—he had nobody and no responsibilities. His time was his, you know what I mean?"

"So?"

"So, since Eddie could get to the records, he started looking up other cases from around '58 that involved Zirelli or anybody connected to him. Pretty soon, it was clear that Zirelli was the guy—you know how? There were three cases from right before and after the Novaks were murdered. Two particular names and faces kept showing up—there were mug shots—and you can imagine what went through Eddie's head when he saw those pictures—they were the two who did the job on his family some fifteen years before."

"Who were these guys?"

"Mike, don't you want to sit down?" Jerry chortled.

Pallison laughed, too. Caught up in Jerry's tale, he had remained standing from the minute he'd arrived. He sat himself in the room's sea-green stuffed vinyl easy chair.

"Who they were didn't matter. Eddie found out they had been killed a few years apart sometime in the sixties. What mattered was that they worked for Zirelli and only Zirelli. No free-lancing. That's how Eddie knew for sure."

"Okay. So Zirelli always went to Luigi's, you said."

Just then, Jerry clenched his bedsheet with both hands, so tight that his knuckles gleamed white. He gritted his teeth. From his depths there came the guttural sounds of unbound agony. In a minute, he released the grip of his right hand and used it to reach for the round brown tube no bigger than what would fit in his palm. With all his strength, it seemed, he gave the tube's black button three pushes with his thumb, and in a moment, lay back his head. Slowly, his whole body relaxed.

"Just give me a second, Mike." Each word was a sentence.

The priest knew not to call the nurse. He had seen many men and women in this stage of their lives, the last one.

In a while, Jerry was ready to resume, ever conscious of the clock. "Once he figured out Luigi's, he told me he began walking in big circles around the restaurant looking for a particular angle. With a little serendipity—the sun's rays hit him as they cut a straight shaft between several buildings—he found a second-rate place called Daryl House. It was two blocks away from Luigi's."

"A hotel?"

"Yeah. You know the kind. They look pretty rundown on the outside, they're never full, but the rooms are okay. With his maintenance uniform, he roamed corridors on the upper floors until he found the right room. He showed up a week later with some BS story about having spent his honeymoon in Room 307, and could he please have it for a few days, for old times' sake?" Jerry laughed out loud. "Eddie said it was so easy he couldn't believe it."

"What was so special about Room 307?"

"Ah-hah!" Jerry weakly pointed upward, signaling the revelation about to come. "The key thing was that the back of the place, or at least part of it, faced right down that alley where the sun pointed him—to the front door of Luigi's."

"Ahhh! So then what?"

"Gee, Mike, you're like a little kid. So, he just camped

until the next day. On Wednesday, he pulled down the shade to where he had raised the bottom window, a foot or so off the sill, and waited."

"Wasn't it still cold out?"

"Nah. Not with steam heat. Those old hotel rooms could get pretty hot."

"So, he gets to see the front door of the pizza place, presumably with binoculars—so what?"

"Sorry, Mike. What I didn't mention earlier—it wouldna made sense then—is that when Eddie was adopted by the Ohio people, they brought him to Huron, the little town I mentioned earlier. It's about fifty miles west of here, right on the lake."

"That would be in the Toledo Diocese. What does that have to do with this, Jerry?" By this time, priest and patient sounded like two guys parked in a Dunkin' Donuts over coffee in the mornings, one telling stories and the other trying to keep the details straight. Each accepted his role.

"Everything. You see, when Eddie lived in Ohio, he was in high school, and where they lived, nearly every boy his age learned to hunt and fish. That's what boys did in those days.

"Okay. Okay. I get it."

"Yeah, well, Eddie became one hell of a shot—you'd almost have to be since you never get to shoot a deer at close range. Is the light going on now?"

"Mmmm. I guess you're going to tell me Eddie shot the guy from two blocks away."

"Yep. Zirelli was late that Wednesday night, but just by

ten minutes or so. Eddie told me that if a few more minutes had gone by, he'd a called it off.

"Why? He had it all set up."

"Because with the sun setting pretty early in a city with tall buildings, the streetlights and lights from the restaurant weren't enough, and he needed as much daylight as possible with the hardware he had."

"Are you going to tell me he did this with an old flintlock from the farm?"

"Haha, Mike." His eyes roamed the room. "All I know is what he told me. It was an old Parker-Hale 270—a British rifle—with a matching scope. He also got holda some sorta sound-muffling device—a big plus since a rifle shot in that concrete canyon woulda sounded like a thunderbolt."

Once again, Jerry grabbed his blanket and gave it a good squeeze with one hand while his other found serenity with the black button on the brown tube. Not to be caught again with even a nanosecond of the jolting pain his pancreas surged to give him, he kept his grip on the device.

"Take your time, Jerry. No hurry."

"Well, maybe not for you, Mike—hah!—but I'm on the clock." Enjoying his own humor, he let his muscles relax a bit before he went on. "As I was saying, Zirelli's car shows up a bit late. He gets out of the back door, passenger side, and starts to walk—probably not more than fifteen feet or so—from the curb to Luigi's front door."

"Meanwhile, Eddie is in the room, rifle ready, right?"

"Right. Lights in the room were off and Eddie's right eye is glued to that scope. Remember, there are a few hundred windows facing that long alley, lights on in some, some dark. Nobody woulda noticed the window of Room 307."

"I see what you mean. Just how long a shot would that have been?"

"About 150 yards, Eddie said. Any further, with the lighting and all, he wouldna been able to pull it off. Did it in one shot, though. Zirelli was wearing a black coat and hat—one of those Kojak-type hats with a little feather in the ropey band—and he bounced as he walked —definitely not like a deer—so the bullet hit him high right in the back center of his hat. Zirelli's hat flew off, as did the top third of his head."

This time, it was Pallison's turn to hold up his hand. "Alright, Jerry. You seem to be enjoying the retelling of this story... ."

"In fact," Jerry cut him off, "I am, Mike—for Eddie's sake. Imagine his satisfaction at finally getting some justice for his family when nobody else wanted ta bother!" Jerry's face was red, his head off the pillow in indignation.

"Jerry, I gotta ask you this question. It's been on my mind since the day we met and you started telling me this story."

"Yeah?" Jerry challenged.

"I hear this line all the time. Somebody comes up to me with the 'I've got this friend' story, and of course, there is no friend. It's them." The priest lowered his voice, making it as gentle as possible. "Jerry, are you Eddie?"

Jerry smiled and could see the surprise on his visitor's face. "I was wondering when you would ask. You ain't heard the end of the story yet, Mike, but no, I'm not Eddie. Eddie was real. He had been carrying his hate and guilt for a long time and wanted to tell somebody, and that somebody was me."

Pallison looked directly into Jerry's eyes. "Okay, Jerry. I'll accept that for now." He looked at his watch. "Before I go, tell me what happened after the shot."

"Eddie said he didn't wait to see. He slowly closed the window, disassembled his rifle and put the parts into his one suitcase."

"And then?"

"Then, he said, he went to bed and had the best sleep he'd had in fifteen years. The next day, he checked out early, took a cab to Penn Station, and took the train here to Ohio."

"My God. That was cold."

Jerry's face hardened. "He got a lot colder, Mike. I guess you have to go?"

"Yes, much as I'd like to hear the end of this whole thing, I'd better get on the rest of my rounds."

"Don't miss next week, Mike."

"I wasn't planning to, Jerry."

"There won't be a week after, I'm thinkin'—so we need to tidy things up."

"I'll be here."

"Can you do the Last Rites for a lapsed Catholic, Mike?"

"Of course I can. We don't call it Last Rites anymore—it's 'Anointing of the Sick.'"

"Have it your way, Mike. For me, it'll be the last rite we do."

~

A week later, Father Pallison walked into the quiet room in a wing the Clinic reserved for those who will never leave. Jerry was still, head back and eyes closed in repose. The priest knew Jerry was alive only because both hands clenched the blanket pulled up around his chest, which moved with a shallow, stuttered cadence.

He looked at the man, shrunken into a weak, helpless form. Was it the disease or the weight of life taking its toll? He sat. Soundlessly, he recited a prayer he knew well, and that he would say again—soon. The words flowed smoothly, "… Lord of Earth we ask that you receive this child into your arms, that he might pass in safety from this crisis. As Thou hast told us with infinite compassion: Let not your heart be troubled: Ye who believe in God, believe also in Me."

Jerry's head was perfectly still, but as if on cue, his eyes opened and searched the ceiling and everything his peripheral vision would allow. Finally, he turned his head and spied his visitor, who at the moment was his only friend in the world.

"Couldn't miss it, eh, Father?"

Pallison smiled. "If you mean your story, Jerry, why yes, it's a grabber. But you know, I have another duty to you, and will do it whenever you are ready."

Jerry's smile in return left a question in Pallison's mind. He wasn't sure if it was one of acceptance of his fate, or some certain knowledge that it was foreordained. He let the thought pass. "You know, Jerry, when we stopped, I had a mitt full of questions for you. For instance, did Eddie simply get away with the murder? He walked out of the hotel without incident? Did you say where he went?"

Jerry forced a chuckle as he and the priest arranged his pillows so he could sit up. "Like I said, he took the train—by then, the Penn Central—and got off in Sandusky. He had taken time off from his job to come back to Huron—Eddie had all of that prearranged. So you're right, Mike, he was cold. And in answer to your first question, yeah, he got away with it. The cops couldn't really tell where the shot came from—too many windows."

"So he stayed in Huron for a while?"

"Couple of weeks, I think."

"And went back to New York? What then?"

Jerry laughed, and coughed. "In my lungs now." He cleared his throat. "Remember *The Honeymooners* with Jackie Gleason and Art Carney?"

"Yeah?"

"Well, Eddie was so scared somebody in the PD might put him together with the Zirelli thing, he got outa there. Paranoid, I guess. There's no way they woulda connected him. Anyway, he put in a bid on another civil service job, and became Ed Norton. So, in answer to your question, he crawled into the sewer like nothin' ever happened."

"But something did happen, you said."

"Yeah. Eddie told me fifty times how good it felt to get Zirelli. So good, in fact, that for a guy with no other vice, he seemed to want one—killin' bad guys."

"I didn't think things happened like that."

"I'm afraid they do, especially if you're not well-centered to begin with. Keep in mind, Mike, Eddie's ballast had shifted many years before. Everybody who knew him thought he was a strange-o. Every attempt at a normal life—except being Ed Norton in the sewer—if ya want to call that normal—failed him. Except, that is, killin' Zirelli."

Pallison nodded. "I'll buy that for now. So, he's back in the city and…?"

"And not a month goes by—this was New York after all—and there's a story on TV about another mob guy weaseling his way out of the chair."

"You mean he was acquitted at trial?"

"No, I mean, the trial was delayed because a key witness suddenly jumped from the Triborough Bridge. So, Eddie simply decided to repeat Plan A, only with a nasty twist." Jerry looked past the priest, expecting to see someone.

"How so?"

"I'll get to that. So, Eddie uses his days to track this guy, Ruben Abramoff, and finds that the guy and his family have a co-op in the East Seventies, not far off Central Park. Listen, Mike, quit lookin' at me like I'm Eddie."

"I'm not, Jerry, but you have to admit you have an amazing memory for details."

"Mike, I've been reciting this story to myself for over twenty years, saving it for this moment."

"Okay, Jerry. Sorry."

"When Eddie scopes out the place, he notices an

amazing thing. Right in front of Abramoff's building, where the canopy comes out over the sidewalk to the curb, there's a manhole cover—not in the center of the street, but just a few feet from the sidewalk."

"I'm not seeing why that's important."

"Father Mike, you ever notice that people tend to pick up on things about other people because of what they do for a living? A barber, for example, probably notices other people's haircuts."

"So?"

"That manhole meant that Eddie could get really close to Abramoff without his boys seein' him comin'. So you almost have to wonder with a guy like Eddie. Did his plan take off because of a nice coincidence, or did it work because he really wanted to kill this guy?"

"But with Zirelli there was a real connection. There was revenge. With this Abramoff guy, there was nothing."

"Exactly! I've asked myself a hundred times if that manhole hadn't been there would things have been different?"

"I see what you mean."

"Pardon me, Mike. You don't see it yet, but you will."

"Go on."

"Well, Eddie thinks about this for a bit, but soon a plan becomes clear. In the maintenance department, there are all kinds of things left from big digs over the years. Equipment, tools, bricks, mortar, you name it."

Pallison remained silent.

"Think dynamite. When Eddie came on, an old guy about to retire was assigned to break him in. You know, give him the tour. So, he shows him all the old underground storage areas. In one of them, he says, 'See, Eddie, a few sticks would really make some noise, eh?'"

"C'mon, Jerry, are you kiddin' me? Dynamite?"

"I wish I could say I was kiddin', Mike. You have no idea."

"So are you going to tell me that Eddie blew this guy up? Right in front of his own house?"

"Yeah." The silence stretched out.

The priest thought Jerry was in pain.

"Sometime in early June," Jerry finally continued, "Eddie got it all figured out—especially learning how to work with dynamite without blowing himself up. One day, when school was out, Abramoff was coming home with his ten-year-old daughter. The limo stopped in its usual spot in front of Sheridan House, where they lived."

"Do I want to hear this, Jerry?"

"You need to, Mike. It's important. The doorman came forward and opened the rear door. Out steps Abramoff and his daughter. Only a few yards away, Eddie musta hesitated a bit with his remote control, but he detonated the five sticks of dynamite just under the manhole cover. The car went sky-high. Metal and fire everywhere." He forced the next words out. "There was nothing left."

"God. They weren't killed?"

"The girl was burned severely, but she lived. Abramoff himself was knocked off his feet and smacked his skull on a concrete pedestal under a giant flower urn. He lived for a few years, a veg. The driver—he didn't make it." Jerry recited the details mechanically, giving the priest the same report he had given himself countless times before.

"Don't tell me he got away with it—again? I can't believe it."

"Eddie was pretty grossed out—just as quickly as the urge to kill came over him, it scared the crap out of him. A week later, he quit his job and left town—he came right back to Ohio and got a job at Cedar Point. Maintenance man, of course."

"So that's the end of it? That's what you were supposed to tell me?"

"Not exactly."

"Good. I don't like that ending. I can feel for Eddie and what happened to his family. I can understand—never condone—what he did to Zirelli. But the rest? No way, Jerry."

"Life doesn't always have good endings, Mike." Jerry's eyes closed. He was tired, and the morphine wasn't doing the job.

"Jerry, you're in pain. I let you get tired. I'm sorry. You want me to go?"

Jerry reached out his hand and grabbed the priest's own. "Father, can you give me a few minutes? Go get yourself a cup of coffee, then come back—we'll complete our business together."

"Our business"? Pallison guessed he meant the Anointing of the Sick. He nodded, and left.

~

"Are you sure you want to go on," Father Pallison asked when he returned. "I can come back, you know, and it doesn't have to be a week."

"I'm good right now, Mike." The words came slowly. "And I'm bettin'," he said, but did not finish the thought. "Besides, I can't go until I have done what I promised to do. It's the only thing keeping me here."

"I'm all ears, Jerry, but you have to satisfy my curiosity. How, for instance, did you and Eddie meet and really, why did he tell you all this?"

"I ran into him one day at the Knotty Pine Tavern in Huron. We sat next to each other at the bar, and one beer led to another. Over a week or more, I heard the whole story."

"I'm not doubting you, Jerry, but that's incredible. Why do you suppose Eddie picked you to tell his story?"

"Well, you know how it is, Mike. Here Eddie commits these murders, one in March, and the others, in June. He comes back to the only place he had known as home, but there's no one here for him. His relatives were dead, and he was such a weird kid, he didn't have any friends from high school."

"I see that."

"Worse, the season was over at Cedar Point, and when the icy winds blow off the lake, it's awfully lonely for some."

"You still haven't answered my question. Why you?"

"Surely you've noticed my accent, Mike. I'm from New York, too, and maybe, he felt he could trust a fellow New Yorker more than anybody else. Strange as it seems."

"Yeah. So what happened to Eddie?"

Jerry looked at his inquisitor, his face expressionless. "I killed him, Mike. That's what happened to him."

Father Pallison, who thought he'd heard everything in his years in the confessional, sat unblinking, not breathing. "You what?!" He could hardly get the words out.

"So now we come to it, Father—why you're here. You didn't come to hear Eddie's story. You came to hear my confession." Jerry winced, as a fist of pain raced up his mid-section and stopped his speech.

When he did not continue, the priest jumped in. "Wait a minute! You said Eddie committed suicide."

"Actually, I never said that at all. That's what other people thought." Jerry paused to let that sink in.

"But why would you kill Eddie Novak?"

"No short answer, there, Mike." Jerry paused. "Let's go back to the Abramoff thing. Remember, I said school was out? For all of his other faults, Abramoff was a decent guy. My wife and I had a little basement apartment about ten blocks further north of the Sheridan. We had only one child, a daughter, Pauline—Paulie we called her—and she was the light of our lives." Tears formed at the corners of his eyes.

"Anyway," he resumed, "Abramoff's little girl, Anna, met our Paulie one day when she came to visit me on the job. They became fast friends despite all the differences— there were very few kids Anna's age in that neighborhood— and from time to time, Anna would have Paulie come for an overnight."

Pallison sat back in his chair, his eyes closed with the pain of anticipation.

"On one particular day, Abramoff and his daughter picked Paulie up in his limo and he was delivering the two to the Sheridan." Jerry stopped and grabbed the metal bed rails.

The priest couldn't tell if Jerry was in pain from the cancer or from the memory that must have eaten at him like acid every hour of every day. "You were…?" Before he could finish, Jerry nodded.

Jerry offered a slight smile. "That's right, Mike, I was the Sheridan's doorman," he said, his voice hardly above a whisper. He paused to let his confessor fully understand. "What I said earlier is all true, exactly as it happened. When I opened the car door and Mr. Abramoff stepped out with his daughter, our little Paulie was still in the back seat of the Lincoln, about to climb out. She didn't make it." Both hands went to his eyes, as if he could hold in the tears and the pain.

He finished replaying the scene. "I caught a glimpse of this guy, off to my left, when I turned to open the door. He had such a faraway look in his eyes, I never forgot it."

"Jerry, I am so sorry about your daughter. And Mrs. Koski? Where is she now?"

"We split up almost right away. The divorce was final two years later. She tried. We tried. But she couldn't be in the same space with me but without Paulie, and she blamed me for encouraging the relationship with the Abramoffs. She assumed what happened had to do with his criminal stuff, and in a way it did, but who woulda thought I was putting Paulie in harm's way?"

"Jerry, it wasn't your fault. So many couples split up when a child dies. It must have been hard for both of you."

"So now you see, Mike. When I knew what I was here for, I couldn't leave this world with it inside me."

"I'm glad you told me," the priest replied, almost in a whisper.

"This may sound strange, Mike, but I feel so much—better!" The syllables came without energy.

"Better?"

"Like I don't have to carry it anymore—any of it. If you need me to go through the ritual, I will, but there's nothing to add. Compared to murder, the rest of my life has been pretty harmless."

"I think we can pass on the usual words from you."

"Thanks."

"Do you mind, though, satisfying my curiosity? I still don't get how you and Eddie connected."

"That was easy, actually."

As Jerry Koski spoke each word, Pallison could see that soon, a good bit of morphine would need to flow into the man to calm him. The priest in him knew that time was becoming precious.

"I was in the hospital for a few weeks after the blast. The cops interviewed me more than once, and I told them about the guy—I had no way of knowing he did it—he just had that weird look. They interviewed a lot of people, and from what they said, I was pretty sure they had talked to the guy I came to know as Eddie Novak."

"But nothing came of it?"

"No. Apparently, he didn't realize the power of the explosion and took some flyin' metal himself—not enough! Later, I found out he was in a bed just down the hall from me at Sinai."

"I still don't understand how you two got together."

"Eddie's not the only one who had revenge as an inspiration. I knew a couple of cops from the station house, and they knew what I—what my wife and I were goin' through. I told them I thought I knew the guy standin' just up the street, but couldn't place him, you know what I mean?" So, before long I had a name and an address. By the time I was able to chase him down, he was gone."

"So how did you find him?"

"That was easy, too. I found the Super in his building—a guy who needed a twenty for some Smirnoffs—and that was the only mistake Eddie made—he asked the Super to forward his mail for a month. He guessed Eddie was waitin' for his last paycheck or the rebate on his rent or somethin'.

"So then I waited. When my wife and I separated, there was nothin' for me, so I took the train to Sandusky—just like Eddie had, it turned out. Huron is a small town, so it didn't take long to catch up with him."

"And?"

"After he told me everything, there was no impulse about it, Mike. It was the only thing in life I wanted to do, but I had no idea I'd have to carry this for so many years."

The priest waited. He knew he would not have to ask.

Jerry's words became labored, a muffled dirge. "In

Huron, there's a long, rocky pier out to the lighthouse. People go fishing there all the time, in all kindsa weather. You know how the lake can be. Shallow—killer storms coming up in a minute. And that's how it happened."

Pallison kept still.

"Nobody saw us, I'm pretty sure. We had a lot to drink. It was cold and drizzling." The words became choppy. "We went out there like a couple of crazies, cast our lines, and waited. The night got worse. Then it happened. The hate, the pain of all the years—it was like a volcano exploding in my head."

We were standing next to each other, and I couldn't help but stare at him through the drizzle. He turned and looking directly into my eyes, he asked, "Just who are you, anyways?"

The priest inhaled deeply, but said nothing.

It was as if all the air whooshed out of the dying man. The pain of the story and the disease overcame him.

"I grabbed him by the front of his jacket, and I had to shout over the storm. I could see the fear in his eyes when I screamed at him, 'I was the doorman, you son of a bitch! You murdered our daughter. Our Paulie.' And then I shoved him."

"Shoved him?"

"Yeah, his back was to the sloping rocks below us. If he slipped on the wet stone, I don't know, but he went backwards. It was dark, but I heard him hit. Hard. An easy way to break a neck."

"What did you do?"

"I scrambled down, feeling my way, until I reached his body. At the water's edge. He wasn't moving."

"He was dead? You didn't say anything to him? Did you do anything for him?"

"No. I couldn't believe I did that. For a minute, I just stood there in the wind and rain, then I just gave him another shove with my foot and he slid all the way in. From the little bit of light coming our way from the lighthouse, I could see the whitecaps pounding away. In a second or two, Eddie was gone."

For a full minute, the two sat in silence.

"Any regret, Jerry?" Pallison asked.

"Honestly?" Jerry's eyes scoured the space in front of him. "I've had so many years to regret killin' that son of a bitch, and for the sake of my soul, I do." He caught his breath. "I'll be answerin' for it, I know, but I can't help feeling better leavin' this world knowing that Eddie's not in it. Him killin' Zirelli was one thing, but the others? My Paulie?"

The priest put his hand on Jerry's shoulder, and waited.

"I told you, Mike, most people would never commit a crime unless…unless the hurt was so deep….I am so sorry." With what little strength he had, he cried.

"It is not my place to judge you," Pallison said lowering his voice. With a tender whisper, he added, "It is my place, however, to help prepare you for the next part of your journey. Shall we do this?"

Jerry nodded, tears streaming in glistening rivulets down his cheeks.

Pallison donned his stole, a purple silk affair emblazoned with the symbol of crucifixion. Blessing Jerry with the sign of the cross, the Latin words of absolution eased into the silence of his thought, "Ego te absolvo…"

As if reading his mind, Jerry asked, "Can you truly forgive my mortal sin, Father?" His voice was starched in pain, yet plaintive, hopeful, while his eyes searched for any other who might have joined them in the room.

"After thirty years as a priest, my friend, I am certain that God will forgive any sin of the contrite, and of Almighty God's love for you," he said gently, "I surely have no doubt."

Carefully, the priest searched his memory for the older words of the rite, as they would be a greater comfort to a man estranged from the church.

Shrinking into himself as Pallison's words commanded the air, the balming sound floated in and out of Jerry's conscious thought.

"…let the fire of the Holy Spirit now descend that this being might be awakened to the world beyond and the life of earth…"

Jerry saw sunny days when he and Paulie crossed the park on Sundays after Mass.

"…I go and prepare a place for you, I will come again, and receive you unto myself: that where I am, there ye may be also…"

Absently, Jerry thumbed the black button of solace.

With the blessed oils, Father Pallison touched Jerry on his forehead, his lips, and his heart. "By this sign, thou art anointed with the grace of the atonement of Jesus Christ and thou art absolved of all past error and freed to take your place in the world he has prepared for us…"

Jerry closed his eyes.

"I have made a covenant with my chosen, I have sworn unto David my servant…"

Paulie came running toward her father.

"And thus do I commend thee unto the arms of our Lord of earth, our Lord Jesus Christ, preserver of all mercy…"

Irina

A young girl, about sixteen, becomes pregnant by the son of the Jewish merchant in whose house she works as a servant. In this instance, young love is true love, but because of racial and religious prejudice, Berek Joselewicz and his entire family are burned alive, blamed for the plague that has just arrived from the east. This story could be told of any era, even today, but Irina Kwasniewska lives in Poznan, Poland. It is 1378, and two forms of the plague have descended upon the city.

The nobles are escaping, and Sister Elizabeth, a Dominican nun, sees to it that Irina, a peasant girl posing as a young woman of minor nobility, becomes attached to Duke Zygmunt's entourage just then leaving for Paris to attend a gathering of Europe's royalty. Soon mentored by the duke's counselor, Father Martinus Madrosh, Irina learns the customs of the wealthy even though Madrosh knows her to be an impostor.

The journey to Paris is months long and dangerous, but the tedious hours on horseback, cart, and barge enable the two to converse on many subjects, principally Irina's denial of God's existence, and the nuances of good and evil. "How can a true God permit so much evil?" she demands. As she is a willing and intelligent pupil, their talks plow fascinating furrows on an old theological landscape.

The journey is not without its dangers, especially to Irina, who is blamed by one of the duke's henchmen—Tomasz Wodowicz—for claiming gold and silver he had intended to steal for himself. His vow to enact a deadly revenge form the backdrop for discussions about good and evil.

What follow are excerpts from their talks from my novel, Irina, *published in 2021.*

~

It is May 1378. Deep in western Poland's Silesian woods, Duke Zygmunt's entourage of some seventy men and women gathers at St. Stephen's monastery to rendezvous with others and replenish supplies. There, Irina, the impostor, meets Father Madrosh, and soon a challenging intellectual relationship develops, sparked by Irina's demands about the Divinity.

"Let me start by suggesting that if there is a God," Father Madrosh says, "one Supreme Being, as it were, he would have to be the essence of perfection, would he not? Flawless in every way. By definition, then, nothing in his creation could equal him because if everything in nature, every living being was perfect, why would he bother. Eh? So, if we are all imperfect in some way, what does that truly mean?"

"Interesting words, Father," Irina responded, "but all the evil around us makes me wonder if there is a God, why does he not care for us?"

"That's exactly it, don't you see? Do you remember the gospel on Good Friday? Christ tells Peter he will deny his master three times. Peter vows he would never do such a thing, but before the cock crows, he denies he even knows the man from Galilee. Yet, despite his flaws, his deep imperfections, Christ says Peter is the rock upon which he will build his church. Think of it!"

Irina nodded. "But Peter was just being human, afraid of what the Jews might do to him if he acknowledged Christ."

"Exactly. We are all human, we are all flawed, and we all fear something."

~

A day further west, the duke's company covers the flat farm lands nearly devoid of human life, over a third of the population having been taken by the Black Death. Irina wants Madrosh to explain why the Jews are being blamed for all the dead and dying. Madrosh provides one answer…

"People always need someone to blame for their calamities. They can't blame God because they're afraid of God. It's much easier to blame people who can't easily defend themselves. And in this case, the church helped to make the Jews seem like evil itself. Even some words in the gospel strengthen that view. When a group is thus identified, it becomes easy to hate them."

~

After many days crossing barren lands, the royal group reaches the Oder River as a vicious storm breaks, and Irina nearly drowns attempting to cross over to Krosno Castle on the other bank—the eastern reaches of German territory. Who saves her is Squire Jan Brezchwa, and over many months, a love relationship enkindles.

"My Lady Irina," Madrosh announced after their midday repast of roast venison and rabbit, a few dried fruits, and a variety of breads. "We should walk, should we not? Let us cross the moat bridge and navigate the square. In your gentle condition, fresh air and a bit of exercise will do you much good."

"As you say, Madrosh, you are now a physician of the body as well as the soul!"

"Since you speak of the soul," he said with a wink, "let us talk more about Thomas Aquinas. He, too, spent much time satisfying himself it was not just by faith alone that one can know God exists. Of course, he believed, fundamentally, that faith alone is sufficient, but for those," and here, Madrosh, cleared his throat, "like you, who want something more substantial before investing in your faith, he offered five proofs of God's existence. Three of them we've discussed somewhat because they are based upon

Aristotle's thinking of over a thousand years before."

"Refresh my memory a bit, won't you?"

"Aquinas focused on the notion of a first and unmoved mover. By this, he did not mean the idea of action as such, but instead, as kinesis—Greek for 'movement'—of potential to actual existence. If you have an idea, for example, it is not the idea itself that makes it real, it is you or someone else—totally separate from the idea. We cannot assume an infinite series of preceding movers without there being something that accounts for the existence of the First Mover. That must be God."

Irina's brow wrinkled. "And?"

"Next, there must be an order of efficient causes—an order without which a series of them cannot take place. We—humans, animals, plants—pass into and out of this world, all dependent on what caused us to be—you would not exist if not for your parents, and they, their parents, and so on. The same is true of plants and animals. The third proof would seem obvious: the very fact that an Original Being must exist leads to the conclusion that this Being is the one and only God."

"That I think I understand."

Madrosh nodded and inhaled deeply before resuming. "Next is a proof drawn from Augustine. His notion of degrees of perfection implies that in the scheme of things, nothing we can see or hold is perfect. Yet, if there is something or some being that is better, then it suggests an even better being beyond, and so on. Should there not, then, be a Perfect Being?"

"I think I see what you mean. When my father carved a wooden bowl for us to use, each was better than the one before it, but none was perfect. Yet, my Berek, the one who is no more, was perfect—to me." She and the old priest strolled across the cobbles and made a circuit of the broad square, busy with shops and the noise of sellers, much like the Fareway in Poznan. She had no interest in the goods offered them—at any price—and kept her focus on the words flowing to her like sips of hot soup on a cold evening.

Madrosh smiled and rested his hand, gently, upon her forearm. "Yes, my Lady, for many, true love is the most perfect of emotions, and your love for Berek, and his for you, was no doubt a very special experience. Yet, as you know your own self not to be perfect, in action or in word," he said, waiting for her nod of acknowledgement, "so too was your Berek, a young man just right for you, but surely not perfect, even if that is how you choose to remember him." His words were forthright, but his voice was as soft as her warm blue blanket. They walked slowly onward.

After a minute or two, he continued. "The last argument has to do with something I said earlier. Our world is not totally random. Just as the Old Testament says God created the world in a particular order, there must be such an order in what we see around us for it to make sense. The foundation of the castle walls is on the bottom, never on the top, you see?

Irina smiled. At the butcher's stall, she stopped and asked for a bit of fat for Yip, who kept them quiet company throughout their saunter. His bushy white tail topped with a black tuft of fur wagged furiously as Irina bent with a treat for her ever loyal friend.

"We'll close this topic with one other idea offered by Aquinas about God. You and I and all other things pass away. Trees rot and disappear, and over time, even stone crumbles. Rivers, too, change course. It is our nature to pass away, and thereby, we change. God's nature does not change. It is always the same. That means that God's nature is, simply, to be."

Irina shook her head, as if dazed by a difficult notion.

"Because we're walking on real ground and not high on the parapets, I can risk making you a bit dizzy with such thoughts," he chuckled. "Here's another: To Aquinas, it was inconceivable for God to have created the world and everything in it out of matter that already existed. If this matter already existed, he wondered, then where did it come from? Aquinas reasoned that in creating the universe, the world as we see it, God would not have done so out of nothing because nothing means there is neither essence nor existence. What made more sense to Aquinas is that God created the first bit of unshaped or unmolded matter, and by sparking it into life, brought forth first our world, the sky, the sun, water, earth, and so on, and more recently, intelligent beings—us."

"Intelligent? I'm not always so sure. Just how far have we really come, good Father?"

"A very good question, Irina." Madrosh paused, taking in her insight. "Do you remember our discussion about free will? God created us and as such, moved his thought into reality, prompting untold 'moves' ever since…"

"What do you mean, Madrosh?"

"Take the notion of God creating the first bit of matter and then, perhaps, and I say perhaps, 'letting it go.' It is much like your father and mother raising you and at the right time, letting you go to make your own life."

Irina's eyes filled with tears. On seeing this, Madrosh quickly added, "I am so sorry, Irina. That was a poor example to use with you. And despite what you told me, my dear, I am certain your mother and father still love you, wherever they may be. In that sense, the example is a good one, my child. You are now operating under your own free will, not that of your parents."

Irina nodded, fighting back many memories.

After a bit, Madrosh continued, "Many in the church talk about free will, but they believe that every single thing that happens is controlled by God, and that we should pray for him to make something happen the way we would wish it, almost as if we're praying for God to change his mind."

"Are you saying, Madrosh, there is no need to pray?"

"On the contrary, Irina. If, indeed, God 'let it go,' then he allows his Creation to grow and blossom like the flowers in the forest. In that case, there is all the more reason to ask him to intervene on our behalf. Sometimes he does and sometimes he answers our prayers by doing nothing at all."

"Now that, Madrosh, is a mystery, is it not?"

"It is one way of saying that because God knows how everything will all turn out, he knows the end of all things—his plan—but he does not make all the things happen in between even though he knows they are happening… More often than not, it is we who make our worlds, not God. Yet, that is why prayer is important because God may intervene for us when it is in keeping with the end he already has in mind for us."

~

The Hungarian army believes Krosno Castle and its inhabitants to be an easy target, especially because Poland's current king is Hungarian, and Zygmunt must remember where his loyalty lies, even if he is the guest of King Wenceslas. Even so, Lady Irina and Father Madrosh continue their talks amid the royal intrigue involving the Poles, Germans, and Hungarians. Irina poses her challenge.

"… Madrosh…my next question is simply this: Is man good or evil?"

"Simply?" Madrosh chortled. "From you, there is no simple question!

"When you ask about good and evil, the answers are many. Great thinkers have pondered these questions for thousands of years. The ancient Greeks, including Socrates, Plato, and Aristotle, were, of course, not Christian in their beliefs. Christ did not exist on earth when these men were living. Augustine was an African who became Bishop of Hippo over 800 years ago, and Thomas Aquinas was an Italian priest who died just about 100 years ago. Different though these men were, they thought and talked much about the idea of a soul, and in consequence, about good and evil. Another large topic! How much do you want me to tell you?"

"Did these foreign men look like us?"

"The Greeks? Yes, they look very much like us, but Augustine was African. He was a black man."

"A black man? I've never seen a black man, or heard of one, for that matter."

"Do you remember the old ones in Poznan and around the farms ever talking about the Mongols? Their skins were much darker than ours, and their features, different as well. Augustine, they say, was even darker, nearly black as soot."

Irina took this in while they climbed to the parapets, where the stonework was just wide enough for the two to walk side by side. The night had been cool, but the morning sun warmed them both. It took away Irina's shiver, allowing her to concentrate on the kettle of knowledge Madrosh was about to pour out for her.

"We have some time today. Tell me a bit about these men, and about our souls."

"Of course, we do not know who might have been the first to talk about it. When Plato wrote about Socrates and his thinking—remember, these men along with Aristotle lived hundreds of years before Christ was born—they talked about the soul as if it were a part of you, but an invisible part.

"They thought you could teach your soul to be what you wanted it to be, wise or foolish, good or evil. They said it is the responsibility of every human being to care for and civilize one's own soul, to seek the good and discover one's path in life. Most interestingly, when the ancients talked about civilizing one's soul, it implied that man is on a continuum of development. That is to say ideas of good and evil may be different now than they were a thousand years ago, and even more so, a thousand years from now.

"Plato used the acorn as an example," he continued. "By itself, it is nothing, just an acorn. The good it must achieve is to become an oak tree, which then might be used to shelter someone or provide a piece of furniture. So, too, must each person seek the good in themselves and bring it to fulfillment."

"I suppose the acorn doesn't know it's supposed to be a tree or a table. Are you answering my question about good and evil? I am confused."

"I am sorry, my Lady. I'm telling you what I understand about this topic because I think you are interested and can comprehend it. Not many of our time, men of the cloth or the sword, have either quality. So, pardon me. You have asked me about things I love to talk about."

Irina smiled. "I would not have guessed." Catching a warming ray of sun, she found a place to sit where the stone had already taken in the heat. She invited Madrosh to share the space from which they could see over the town and across the river, well into the distance. Yip, who never left her side, lay down at her feet, the warm stone a welcome treat for the old dog. Irina studied him for a moment, wondering if Yip had a soul, and would he find his purpose, like the acorn? "Since you don't mind my questions, my wise Madrosh, please continue."

"As you wish, Lady Irina. It was Aristotle who took their thinking further. He believed that neither the soul nor the body can exist without the other. He felt that all behavior is guided by its own end—a particular good."

"Just what good is Tomasz the Terrible seeking, Father Madrosh?!"

"One must wonder. Yet, we have to believe good will come of Tomasz's evil." Madrosh paused to let that thought find its way to Irina's keen mind and find rest there. He continued. "It is thought that Aristotle proposed the notion of a First Cause, but he was not necessarily talking about God. He recognized the necessity of there being a First Cause, but he considered it to be defined as eternal thought—a rather complex idea! Perhaps I am wandering too far into deep waters."

"So if I could sum up these three thinkers," Irina ventured, "it sounds like they were attempting to find a reason for our existence, perhaps seeking a purpose for us. And they thought it was our duty to seek the good in whatever we did or became."

Madrosh sat silent. Smiling in appreciation of her mental acuity, he said as much. "But in this regard, they could take all their brilliance no further, my dear. It was not until Christ came on earth that it all began to make some sense."

~

At his peril, Zygmunt opts to support his host, King Wenceslas, and together, they outwit the Hungarians, luring the attackers into a deadly trap. To a man, they are slaughtered as Irina and Madrosh watch from the parapets above them. Horrified at the carnage, seemingly perpetuating the evils she witnessed in Poznan, she challenges Madrosh anew about God and the eternal battle between good and evil. Madrosh considers the topic before him...

Warming to the topic on Irina's mind, Madrosh cleared his throat. "I want to mention Aristotle's thinking about the soul. He is said to have believed that when a baby is conceived, it has a vegetative soul, that is, the essence of a senseless entity. When the baby grows a bit, it receives an animal soul, and finally, when it achieves its humanity, a rational soul."

Irina gave him a look of impatience.

Madrosh held up a finger to forestall her complaint. "Just a moment, my dear. I must add that Aristotle went on to say that the human soul is then divided into the rational and irrational. The irrational, in turn, is part vegetative—reason cannot control it—and animal—it has appetites but is controllable. The rational soul has the capability of understanding complex thought and making moral judgments."

Madrosh let the thought settle, and continued. "One might say—and this may or may not be exactly what Aristotle said—that everyone has a rational and irrational soul, but each person has one or the other in differing amounts or degrees. Do you see where that thought might take us?"

She said nothing.

"I mention this to explain why in our time many men

of the church, even Augustine, have not objected greatly to the deliberate loss of an unborn baby." He said this and lowered his eyes.

"What are you trying to tell me, Madrosh?" Her voice was nearly a whisper.

"At the present time, many in the church condemn the sin of sex outside of marriage, but not a deliberate miscarriage, as long as it happens before the baby becomes ensouled."

"Are you suggesting that I find a way to miscarry, Madrosh?" Irina felt color rising in her cheeks. "Is this your way of telling me it would be better, more convenient for me?" she demanded, anger claiming each syllable of her words. "Do you not yet understand what I am about? Would I have gone to this extreme," she said, extending her arms to show where they were, how far they had come, "to rid myself of a child I did not want?"

"I am so sorry, my Lady," the old counselor hastened to say. "Truly, I admire you for not having done what many have done, all with the forgiveness of the Church."

"Madrosh, understand me now! This baby means everything to me, and I will carry it as long as God wants it so. This child also carries Berek's spirit, and that I will never forget."

"I understand perfectly," Madrosh said, realizing he had touched a most tender spot in Irina's emotional well-being.

The spring air became heavy with their silence. Irina swallowed hard. Finally, in an attempt to put the exchange aside, she asked, "Are you saying that how each person's soul is made up determines whether a person is good or evil?"

"That could be one answer, yes, Irina"

"Might you be saying, then, that a creature like Tomasz may have very little of a rational soul?"

"That may be what the Greeks would say. As Christians, we have a different view of the soul.

~

Departing Krosno Castle by barge and traveling up the Oder, Duke Zygmunt's party having joined that of King Wenceslas, their barges eventually take them to where they can easily make their way to Tangermunde in July, bypassing the small village of Berlin. There they are met by another King Charles, the Holy Roman Emperor. Ever persistent, Irina prods her mentor to say more about what she knows so little. Madrosh begins...

"Let's talk about the good Augustine, then, and the opposites of good and evil."

It was amazing to her how he could change his demeanor in an instant. No wonder the duke prizes him as his counselor, she thought.

"The question often arises, Lady Irina, if God knows that evils will occur, is he God? If God does not know, how can he be God? And if he knows, and does nothing, is he a God without power? Or an uncaring God? And if he has no power or does not use it, how, too, can he be God?"

Madrosh had wasted no time laying out the challenges

to the very essence of the Creator. Irina nearly regretted having asked the question. "You are making me dizzy, Madrosh!"

"I apologize, my Lady. Free will can be dizzying. You see, it is not God who does and permits evil, it is man. When you lived on the farm and your mother left butter and sugar on the table, she probably told you not to touch it. She knew, however, that you would be tempted, and that when she was not looking, you might take a taste with your finger."

Irina suppressed a guilty giggle.

Madrosh laughed. "Do you remember, Irina? Whether you tasted it or not, your mother did not make either choice for you." He paused. "God knows about Franciszek and Tomasz, but he does not make them do what they do, and we earnestly believe God will hold them accountable for all their deeds! Augustine further believed that once one knows the truth, one is responsible for the truth."

Irina interrupted. "Forgive me, Madrosh, if I am speaking sinfully, but what does God think of Bishop Tirasewicz?"

Madrosh laughed heartily. "I do not know what God thinks of him, my child, but Augustine gave us some thoughts on this as well. He believed that it is Christ only who determines whether a sacrament is valid. That means that when our bishop performs a baptism or a marriage, or forgives someone's sins in Christ's name, his behaviors, as we may judge them, are separate from the acts he performs on Christ's behalf." After a moment of reflection, he added, "That is not an easy garment to don, is it? It is a simple reminder for us that while we may make our own judgments about someone, in the end, it is solely the judgment of God that matters."

"And in the end," she taunted Madrosh, "is man judged good or evil?"

"You have heard the ancients and you have heard me. The ancients believed that man is intrinsically good—that all natures are created by God and therefore, could not be evil in themselves. There are some who think God may have created Adam and Eve as innocents, as intrinsically good, but because of their sin, we are born with varying degrees of good and evil in us—you'll remember we spoke of this earlier."

"What is this word, 'intrinsic'?"

"It means the very core of something. Deep inside an apple, the very center of it has the seeds for another of the same, and those seeds have within them the power to grow an apple tree that produces apples, sweet or sour—the vegetative soul, remember? What's in the heart or core of the apple is not what we see by its skin, but it is what makes the apple what it is. Underneath, where you cannot see or touch, is this essence—our nature.

"Think about it this way," he went on. "If man, king or servant, is born with evil in his soul, but overcomes it by his free will, then he will become the person we may not want to judge harshly. If a man overcomes his evil desires and seeks what is good, is that not what God wants?

"What about someone who seems by nature a good person?"

"God may judge such a person on a different plane. One has to think that a person who has not been tempted by sin cannot claim virtue."

"I see."

"Think about man from our earliest history. Have his urges been to benign behaviors or have they tended toward the evils of greed, covetousness, lust, and murder? God's gift to Moses of the Commandments helped to civilize our souls. God's gift to us of his Son helps to educate our souls to choose what is good."

"So God judges us by what we do with our lives, not by what we are at our borning."

"Well said, Irina."

~

"Let us go back to Augustine's insight about natural law in the Garden of Eden. He said it was there that natural law existed in its purest form, as a model of perfection, perhaps, but when man was expelled from Paradise, it was no longer possible to live according to the law."

"Yes, that's what I understood you to say."

"That's true as stated—and by the way, my dear Irina, what I have said to you about the philosophers and the view of the church is all my understanding of their teachings. If someday you learn that I spoke erroneously, I do hope you will forgive this old man."

"You were saying…as you approach the hangman?" She laughed merrily.

"It is not you dangling there, my dear! What I was saying was if Augustine's insight is correct, it means that even in Paradise, man's nature, which we thought had been incorrupt and incorruptible, compelled him to grasp what was not his—the apple of eternal wisdom.

"Do you see? If even in a state of grace in God's special Garden, a place where Adam and Eve wanted for nothing, if even in such a place, man's nature prevailed over the so-called perfection of natural law, then man never had a perfect nature at all.

"He was never destined to live in Paradise because God knew that with Adam's free will, he would defy God's commandment about the forbidden fruit. God knew all along that Adam and Eve would leave and propagate the earth. The Almighty didn't make it happen, but he knew it would happen. Some would interpret those events as God's plan, after all."

"Madrosh, how can you be condemned for this thinking?"

"You must take it a step further, Irina. Aristotle, Plato, Augustine, Aquinas, Christian and non-believers alike, have all held that at base, man's nature is good, always seeking the good. Remember our talk of the soul—the acorn that must grow into an oak?"

"And you believe what?"

"There are only two other possibilities. Man is by nature evil, or man is by nature neither good nor evil."

"And so, Master Madrosh, what are we?"

"One is easily tempted to think of man's nature as evil.

When you consider that from the beginning of time, man has controlled his impulses only when under the forceful eye of another, that fact is telling. Only when men formed into groups for protection and the peace which comes from kinship did he learn he could not do whatever he wanted with whomever he chose. He was no longer free to take any woman for his own, to take another man's animal, to kill or rob—when those transgressions were made against those in his group. These rules did not apply—and still do not, as we can see daily—when the women, the animals, or possessions belong to another group." Madrosh paused so that she could think about what he'd said, then continued.

"And in each group, who rules? The strongest, the biggest, the one others will support with arms and fealty—and the one they will fear."

"I'm not sure I understand your conclusion," Irina said.

"From ancient times, kings imposed rules of their own making. These could be laws about how a man goes about buying a goat, how he must pay his taxes, and so on. Laws would be made without relevance to God or religion. Rarely was there a moral underpinning of right and wrong until the Commandments came to Moses."

"And those same Commandments have been used in conquering and killing other peoples, Madrosh!"

"Exactly. A group with Commandments is sometimes no different than a group without them."

"So, if you believe that man is basically evil, why would God create us?"

"Another marvelous question, Irina! Yet, I did not say

that man is evil—it is, merely, one possibility. We are now led to the proposition that man is neither good nor evil. Upon reflection, I would contend that every man is born different, his stewpot having varying proportions of good and evil in it. And yes, he is a child of God, made with all the potential to be in the image of God. The man grows up to be what he wants to be—good or evil or likely, at times, one or the other—in spite of his parentage and upbringing. You yourself know of persons like Sister Mary Elisabeth and Tomasz the Terrible—both children of God, yet one grew to be decidedly good, and the other, decidedly evil."

"If God is just, how could he judge a man or woman if they were raised to steal and kill, if that's all they knew in life?"

"God is just, my dear, and it is my belief that in his truly infinite wisdom He judges each of us based on what we were born to, and later, how we were able to exercise our free will. The most important words here are 'how we were able.'"

"Do you think God gave us the Commandments and, later, Christ his Son, to balance the evil in the world?"

"From time's first flash of light until July in the Year of Our Lord 1378, we haven't come very far, have we? If man is by nature good, the Joselewicz family would never have encountered the terrible Tomasz." Madrosh exhaled, obviously relieved that at last, he had spoken his notions aloud.

Irina observed the priest carefully. Had he just made an act of confession?

Madrosh smiled to himself, adding for her ears, "And

yet, my dear. God always seems to offer us a way to save ourselves."

~

By November, the travelers reach Paris, having traversed western Poland, much of Germany, and parts of France. There, Irina is introduced to the court of France's King Charles, and to the political maneuverings surrounding the existence of two Popes, one at Avignon and one in Rome. The machinations eventually become personal to Irina and her husband, Jan Brezchwa, when her life and family are threatened from on high, and when Tomasz Wodowicz, thought to be dead, appears to exact his revenge.

Irina's entire story is available on Amazon.

The Christmas Kid

Originally published in the Winter 1997 edition of Buffalo Spree *magazine, this true story, edited slightly, is presented publicly for only the second time.*

Dad! It's time!" Rob called with impatience. Not even an hour home from church, and already my twelve-year-old had begun his campaign.

Placidly, I sat at the dining room table with coffee, a buttered Kaiser roll, and the *Sunday Post-Gazette*, Pittsburgh's one and only, and all I wanted was thirty minutes of peace.

"Time for what?" I asked with parental innocence and preoccupation.

"You know!" he responded, his tone carrying with it the weight of having been born to a father hopelessly incapable of intelligent conversation. "This is the day. You said we'd put up Uncle Paul's trains."

"Okay. Give me a few minutes." He turned away, dejected, but I knew he'd be back. At our house in northwestern Pennsylvania, arranging a large oval of Uncle Paul's trains around our Christmas tree would become a fast tradition, and for Rob, it marked what was an already bounteous season of wonder and miracles. My son respected the trains, their value, and their meaning to us both, and this year more than any other, he suspected, would be different. Though we would select the many pieces together, he knew that I would let him set it all up himself, handling the engines, the wiring, the transformer, everything.

How much Rob was like my only brother, I thought as I glanced out the oversized, mullioned windows. Heavy, wet snowflakes fell straight down, whitening the ground and fulfilling the weatherman's prophecy. My mind strayed from the *Post-Gazette* to earlier times.

~

In my growing-up years, Paul was the Christmas Kid in our family. From the time he was little, my parents told me, Paul was enthralled by Santa, the lighted, tinseled tree, and his first electric train, an American Flyer given him by his godfather in 1941. Outside lights, decorations abounding, carols and cookies, and Midnight Mass—all were a glorious whole making the winter days long and bright. Although he never forgot Christmas was about the Christ Child, for Paul, as it was for many boys, it was the earthly reality of the electric train that sparked his childhood fantasies in that most delightful season.

When I came along, and was old enough, I was allowed to accompany him on the annual visit to Spoonley the Trainman's shop in Buffalo, New York, where we grew up. All year long, my big brother saved his "paper money," which he earned delivering the *Buffalo Evening News*, so that he could build his dreams, a piece at a time, from Spoonley's well-stocked shelves. The store was a veritable roundhouse full of orange and blue boxes, a sign of Lionel playgrounds everywhere, and I stood, wide-eyed in admiration, as he made his choices for the year. Each visit was an hour or two of pure boyhood heaven.

~

"Ready, Dad?" Rob asked as he passed through to the kitchen. His voice brought me back to the present, and I had to admit, he'd been patient. The outside decorations had been installed by early December. Then my wife, Beth, and I, Rob, and his sister, Rebecca, performed the loving task of festooning the house with every bit of Christmas we dared to show. Last, of course, came the tree, and that we hoisted and decorated on Friday, two weeks before Christmas itself. The setting was nearly complete.

Rob didn't wait for me to respond. Masterful tactician that he can be, he put together the right words to move my spirit. "Dad," he said, "do you know why I like to put Uncle Paul's trains around our tree?"

I bit. "Why?"

"Because when we do, it's like he's here with us."

That did it. Coffee and paper aside, we went to the basement, sifted through the mountain of boxes, and made our choices for the year. Up he went with his junior partner, Rebecca, in tow. In minutes, they were busy in the living room, and for their eyes, a great railroad was soon to take shape. The tracks, the signals, the buildings, the cars, and their beloved leaders, the Lackawanna and the New York Central.

Back in my own Sunday spot, I traveled back to boyhood. It was in 1956, I remembered, that Paul paid the princely sum of $67 on Lionel's big new engine, the Lackawanna, a shining brute of a diesel in beautiful gray, maroon, and yellow livery. It was not easy for my very practical parents—people of modest means—to let him spend that kind of money, but they knew he had worked hard, and for him, trains were everything.

In the years to come, Paul's railroad empire grew and I became his partner—the junior one, of course—and we continued our tradition of setting up the boards every Christmastime. Whole towns and rail yards transformed our bare basement into every boy's dreamland of unlimited possibilities for pint-sized adventure. From Thanksgiving to New Year's, it was our once-a-year opportunity for seemingly endless days of trainboard activity supercharged by the electricity of the season and our own imagination.

By the early sixties, Paul and I had pooled our resources to buy another engine, this time a used New York Central diesel pair, but because its horn no longer worked, it became the Lackawanna's silent companion on our layout.

Yet, it was a gorgeous, gleaming wonder of a passenger engine, which could pull a dozen cars up any grade on any table. One January, in our haste to pack it all away, one of us forgot to remove the battery from the Lackawanna's underside, and of course, by the following December, the acid had done its dirty work. Now, too, it stood in mute testimony to our love of the trains, and like the two engines, Paul and I were never to be the same.

1967 was the last time we put up the trains as a team. Soon, I was off to the Army and Paul, to another city. As brothers sometimes do, we grew away and apart, and only a few times a year did we cross paths, usually before the end of December. As always, we talked about layouts gone by, but even Paul, his love for Christmas never lost, had put aside his railroading dreams as the realities of life and livelihood intervened.

When Rob was born, we asked Paul to be his godfather. To no one's surprise, Paul gave him his first toy trains, and though the three of us were linked by blood and the love of a boy's pastime, it seemed there was something more between Paul and his only nephew. Much to our annual amusement, Rob spent hours lying in front of the Christmas tree, entranced by all that lit the days and weeks of the Yuletide. His love of trains and Christmastime grew, not in any way diminished by encroaching maturity or the distractions of other seasons.

~

At first, the noise gave me a start. It was only the clackety-clack of the great engines lumbering over their carpeted roadbed, after all. The kids were having fun. And in a way, so was I. With another cup of coffee in hand, I hurried back to memories of someone I hadn't spoken to in a while.

By the late 1980s, Paul had once again immersed himself in the great Lionels, and was well on his way to completing a new layout for his old engines. Always on a budget, he found a repairman who, for a reasonable price, overhauled the venerable Lackawanna and the NYC, but despite their renewed beauty and the hum of their motors, their mighty horns weren't worth what it would cost to fix them.

Along the way, Paul made sure to further Rob's interest in their mutual love. An unlikely pair of railroad veterans, he and his godson talked trains whenever they were together. In the years that followed, Rob's whole attention turned to trains from the last bite of November's pumpkin pie to the last gulp of New Year's eggnog.

The seasons gave us new rounds of beginnings and endings. Increasingly ill from the complications of Crohn's Disease, Paul made sure I knew that were his time to come, there wouldn't be much in his estate but "the trains, and they were for Rob." We didn't anticipate his promise being fulfilled as quickly as it was. After the next Thanksgiving together at Mom's, we left in opposite directions, but within a week, I rushed to say goodbye as Paul breathed his last in a Cleveland hospital bed. At fifty-one, his sudden departure meant that never again would we design new towns, lay straight the rails, wire the switches, or test our work together.

Beth and I didn't tell Rob about the legacy until the following summer when as father and son, we made our pilgrimage to Paul's home, and there began the bittersweet duty of dismantling his last dream. Ten-year-old Rob fully appreciated our task, and together, we tenderly wrapped the vast numbers of cars, track, switches, operating devices, and a whole city of buildings and their miniature inhabitants. It had been a good experience for us, one we've not forgotten.

~

Lost as I was in my own reverie, it took a moment before I consciously recognized another sound coming from the living room. Then it hit me. It was the clear, brilliant, electric blast of the Lackawanna's long-stilled horn hitting a note I hadn't heard in over twenty-five years. With a tingle up my spine, I got up from the chair, savoring each repetition of the horn's sound as it cheered my way toward the Christmas tree.

"Rob," I said, incredulously, "what did you do? How did you get the horn to work?" As a matter of ritual, we had tried to give it voice every year, Rob and I, and decades before that, Paul and I. All we had ever achieved was the hollow click of an electrical contact sparking nothing.

"Don't know, Dad. I just decided to put in a battery and turn the switch," he answered with satisfaction and glee, as he put the great train through its paces and sounded its song every few seconds.

The awful impossibility of the Lackawanna's new voice made me recall another strange occurrence, quietly put aside a few years earlier. When Rob and I made our trip to western Ohio in the summer of '92, we had dropped Rebecca at my mother's house, halfway, and gone on alone. On the way over, one of the tires on the car had seemed out of alignment, but not otherwise troublesome as we journeyed back to Mom's house, loaded down with cartons of train equipment. Rob and I checked the tires repeatedly and, I thought, thoroughly, but found nothing.

The next day, Mom and Rebecca joined us for the last 150 miles home via I-80. Noticeably, our speed was slowed by a wheel acting out of sync with the rest of the car. Twice we stopped and checked, and saw nothing. We drove very slowly, like Depression-era emigrants prosperity-bound, and finally made it home.

At our local garage, the mechanic showed me the problem: a lemon-sized bubble on the inside sidewall, unnoticeable to the average driver—like me—unless I happened to be looking right at it. When I told the mechanic of our previous day's travel, he gaped in amazement.

"You are one lucky man! A few more miles and this would have blown. I don't know how you made it."

Neither did I, but I had the sense to look heavenward and give proper thanks. I even permitted myself to wonder if it were possible for Paul to have had a hand in protecting us during our journey for him and his beloved trains, but the realist in me finally let it rest on the shelf of Providence or plain, good fortune.

Until Sunday afternoon, just before Christmas. Rob shook me back to the living room and the layout before us. "Dad, what do you think? Should we try the New York Central's horn?"

Still a prisoner of unrelenting practicality, but having learned not to shake a boy's faith, I chuckled and said, "Well, Rob, go ahead, but you might be pushing your luck just a little."

In the flash of time it takes the average boy to put a D-Cell in its proper place, the old NYC trumpeted its presence in our midst. To my utter disbelief, the thirty-five-year-old engine, never heard before by any of us, including Uncle Paul himself, began to sing its stark song for us, as warm and reverent an audience as could be. Rob's unquestioning assurance, his complete faith in the impossible, was there for all of us to see—and hear.

Oh, I know there could be any number of reasons why a dangerous tire didn't blow on the highway when, by all rights, it should have. And I know there are any number of reasons why corrosion in an old electrical device could suddenly shake loose and give it life. I suppose, even, it could happen to two old train engines at the same time for the first time in decades. I know all that.

But maybe none of those practical possibilities ever actually occurred at all. Maybe, just maybe, a wonderful brother and loving godfather simply wanted to announce his presence to us in a way we would understand—just so he could spend one more beautiful Season celebrating the miracle with us, and especially with Rob, another Christmas Kid.

Western Pennsylvania local venue make this a hard-to-put-down novel.

MURDER DOWN DEEP

~ I felt like a third member of the detective team of Fletcher Strand and Joe Bentsen as they methodically went about unraveling how dead bodies kept showing up in an underground mine. …Each chapter adds to the mystery and makes it difficult, if not impossible, to stop reading.

....

~ Murder Down Deep is an excellent sequel to Winter's Dead….Character development is pitch perfect.

....

~ Very intricate web in this mystery. The story is very believable with all the real locations in this rural area of Western Pennsylvania with Amish, underground mine, and small town flavor. Just could not stop reading.

....

~ Fletcher jumps off the pages! I loved the descriptive areas, people, everything! Been waiting for this 2nd book...bring on the 3rd!!!!

....

WINTER'S DEAD

FINALIST! "Winter's Dead is one of the year's best thrillers." – BestThrillers

~ A quick and fascinating read…really was difficult to put down…unexpected twists and turns from the first page to the very last.

~ A great mix of characters and the descriptive language suck you into the life of Pennsylvania coal country. A book that's hard to put down.

....

~ Well written and fast moving with a strong message about child abuse and neglect. An ending I didn't see coming.

....

~ If you enjoy murder mysteries, you'll surely enjoy this offering…extremely well written and keeps you "on your toes" throughout…I'll look forward to the next Fletcher Strand novel.

....

~ I read Irina, *which I thoroughly enjoyed…I absolutely got hooked by* Winter's Dead, *finished in 2 days. I hope it becomes a series.*

....

~ The characters are interesting and the winter scene is done well.

....

~ An intriguing mystery with twists and turns that kept me wondering "whodunit" until the end. A memorable array of characters.

....

~ I got into this story right away…would rank Winter's Dead *as top notch, can't wait for the next book in the Strand series.*

IRINA

~ Irina is a captivating story of love, hope, pain, and perse-verance. I didn't want to put the book down…I found my-self thinking of the characters and the stories. I was obsessed with the intertwining story lines…Irina was spellbinding, the character and the novel.

....

~ This book was like listening to myself at the age of 12, start-ing my own journey, asking all the same questions…Felt good…Amazing research.

....

~ Irina is a wonderful tale of triumph and courage during a difficult time in history…writes beautifully and masterfully weaves several story lines together. Highly recommended.

....

~ A first rate look at life in turbulent Poland in the 14th cen-tury…excellent character development and an absorbing story of a woman's reinvention of herself in Medieval France.

....

~ Irina took me on an emotional journey both beautiful and lyrical from the first few pages. I could not put it down.

....

~ This is the type of saga that I'd love to see as a mini-series! From beginning to end, it was so well developed and at the same time, emotional. I particularly enjoyed the way Mr. Warren gave detailed information on how to pronounce the names! I have recommended this novel to everyone!